My Glimpse of
ETERNITY

My Glimpse of
ETERNITY

BETTY MALZ

Chosen

a division of Baker Publishing Group
Minneapolis, Minnesota

© 1977 by Betty P. Malz

Published by Chosen Books
11400 Hampshire Avenue South
Bloomington, Minnesota 55438
www.chosenbooks.com

Chosen Books is a division of
Baker Publishing Group, Grand Rapids, Michigan

Library of Congress Cataloging-in-Publication Data is available for this title.

ISBN 978-0-8007-9066-0

Printed in the United States of America

12 13 14 15 16 17 18   7 6 5 4 3 2 1

This book is dedicated to
everyone who needs a miracle

CONTENTS

ACKNOWLEDGMENTS

To Len LeSourd for the months of hard work and professional "know how" he invested . . . taking my raw material and refining it into digestible reading. His shepherding and tutoring have been to me a journalism course I could not have afforded.

To Catherine Marshall for her "reader's digest form" of my story that got my writing career "off the ground" ("A Glimpse of Eternity," May 1976 of *Guideposts*).

To Carl, my husband, for keeping his hand in the middle of my back, sometimes patting, sometimes pushing.

To my gracious mother-in-law, Dorothy Upchurch . . . for her patience with me during the long years of my immaturity, and for allowing me to express and confess about *us*.

FOREWORD

MY FIRST KNOWLEDGE of Betty Malz came through a pamphlet mailed to me by a stranger. The story it contained riveted my attention. Betty's experience seemed like nothing so much as a modern version of the raising of Jairus's daughter (Mark 5:22–24, 35–43); it was so spectacular that it defied credibility. I knew then that I would have to investigate it all the way.

Correspondence with Mrs. Malz eventually resulted in a date set for a visit with us at Evergreen Farm in Virginia. "May I bring my daughter April with me?" she wrote.

A few days later as the passengers from Houston steamed through the gates at Dulles International Airport, Len and I immediately spotted Mrs. Malz and her daughter. Tall and willowy-slim, with clear eyes in a face alive with the joy of life, Betty is still a young and attractive woman. The delightful nine-year-old with long blonde hair, two steps ahead of her mother, opened with, "Do you have any horses on your farm?"

Laughingly, her mother explained, "April has a passion for all animals. She wants to be a veterinarian when she grows up."

Later that evening, while April was outside happily making friends with Toby and Gretchen, the two dogs, and Spooky, the cat, her mother settled down to talk. And then I heard from Betty's own lips the story of her amazing experience.

It happened when she was twenty-seven years old. In the Union Hospital of Terre Haute, Indiana at 5 a.m. on a July morning, 1959, Betty was pronounced dead, a sheet pulled over her head. The Lord had awakened her father, the Rev. Glenn Perkins, at 3:30 that morning and had told him to take the forty-minute drive back to the hospital. It was part of God's master plan that Betty's father was to be standing by his daughter's bed to see for himself the drama about to take place.

In *My Glimpse of Eternity*, Betty Malz describes her experience on the other side of that dividing line that we call "death," and how she returned to her body on the hospital bed—to the stunned amazement of her grieving father and the hospital personnel.

"You make dying sound like good news," her husband John later told her after listening to her experience.

This book *is* good news for all of us whose mortality haunts us.

Upon occasion God breaks into human life to give us a glimpse of what lies ahead for us. Betty Malz's remarkable experience is a resounding "Yes, there *is* life after death." More than that, "Yes, God is real and does, in our time, still have power over life and death."

Yet *My Glimpse of Eternity* is even more than that. For it is the story of how God dealt with a proud, materialistic, controlling woman who had to die to learn how to live.

Here is a ringingly triumphant book, a love letter from the Lord of glory to each one of us.

Catherine Marshall
Evergreen Farm
July 5, 1977

PROLOGUE

THE TRANSITION WAS serene and peaceful. I was walking up a beautiful green hill. It was steep, but my leg motion was effortless and a deep ecstasy flooded my body. I looked down. I seemed to be barefoot, but the complete outer shape of my body was a blur and colorless. Yet I was walking on grass, the most vivid shade of green I had ever seen. Each blade was perhaps one inch long, the texture like fine velvet; every blade was alive and moving. As the bottoms of my feet touched the grass, something alive in the grass was transmitted up through my whole body with each step I took.

"Can this be death?" I wondered. If so, I certainly had nothing to fear. There was no darkness, no uncertainty, only a change in location and a total sense of well-being.

All around me was a magnificent deep blue sky, unobscured by clouds. Looking about, I realized that there was no road or path. Yet I seemed to know where to go.

Then I realized I was not walking alone. To the left, and a little behind me, strode a tall, masculine-looking figure in a robe. I wondered if he were an angel and tried to see if he had wings. But he was facing me and I could not see his back.

I sensed, however, that he could go anywhere he wanted and very quickly.

We did not speak to each other. Somehow it didn't seem necessary, for we were both going in the same direction. Then I became aware that he was not a stranger. He knew me and I felt a strange kinship with him. Where had we met? Had we always known each other? It seemed we had. Where were we now going . . . ?

1

THE WARNING

THROUGH THE HALL window I saw my mother-in-law walking up to the front door, suitcase in hand. With a low moan I realized that John had done it again. He had invited his mother for a visit and had forgotten to tell me. It could not have come at a worse time. John, our daughter Brenda, and I were getting ready to go on vacation. Drawing a deep breath, I opened the door with a smile of welcome.

Mother Upchurch dropped her suitcase on the hall rug and looked around. There was severity in the way her jet-black hair was done up in a bun on the back of her head. The strong set of her jaw was somehow heightened by the mole in the middle of her chin. Her probing dark brown eyes mirrored a sharp and active mind.

"New drapes?" she asked, pointing to the living room.

I nodded and braced myself for the question I knew was coming.

Dorothy walked into the living room and studied the drapes for a moment before slipping behind the long davenport to feel their texture. "They go well with the furniture," she said, approvingly, as she studied the red, white and black color motif of the room. "How much did they cost?"

I sighed. "Less than you would believe." Then I turned the conversation to something else, irritated that I had to give so many evasive answers to her questions about how much John and I were spending on our possessions. My replies ranged from a terse "not much" to "about half of what it was worth" to "an unbelievable bargain."

Sensing my annoyance, Dorothy retrieved her suitcase and quickly headed for the guest bedroom where she always stayed, leaving me to fight down my guilty feelings. Dorothy Upchurch, despite her probing manner and unannounced visits, was not a selfish person. Her appearance in the home of her children always meant pans of fresh cookies, succulent baked dishes, washing, mending, ironing—the giving of herself to dozens of small tasks. She deeply cared for the members of her family. If only she weren't so efficient and so often right in her observations and evaluations.

Later that afternoon, before John came home from work and Brenda returned from a playmate's house, Mother revealed her primary concern as we sat drinking coffee at the kitchen table.

"John is working too hard," she began.

"John has always worked hard," I replied. "No one can slow him down."

"You can," she said, her intense eyes drilling holes through me.

It was a tired, familiar conversation. John had been sick with rheumatic fever as a boy. A heart murmur resulted but doctors couldn't agree as to whether there was heart damage, or if so how much. Meanwhile, John had grown up intensely competitive in athletics, an outdoor man who loved hard work as the manager of a Sunoco service station in our home town of Terre Haute, Indiana.

Dorothy sipped her coffee and kept her eyes on me. "The work he does at the station doesn't worry me so much as the financial pressure he's under," she continued.

"What financial pressure?" I asked, fighting down irritation.

"The pressure to pay for a new car, a new boat, and now I understand you're thinking of building a new home," she said.

I bit my lip to keep from lashing out at my mother-in-law. Why did she meddle so much in our affairs? Emotions under control, I tried to explain that we were not reckless spenders, that John knew how to manage money.

But Dorothy doggedly returned to the issue of her son's health. "I know in my spirit that John will have a heart problem unless you slow him down," she said, her lips tightly pursed together.

Dorothy made her visit a short one when she learned we were getting ready to go on a vacation. Her concern for John's health nagged at me for several days until I firmly decided that my mother-in-law was a negative thinker about her son. I was not going to dwell on death, but life. At twenty-nine, John's vitality seemed endless. We loved sunshine, water, boats, convertibles, tennis, music. At twenty-seven, I felt so glowing with good health that I could not recall being sick in bed for even one day of my life.

And yet my physical death was only weeks away!

The morning before we were to leave for our two-week Florida vacation, my husband began the day on the run as usual. Still buttoning his shirt, John slid into the turquoise leather breakfast bar of our kitchen and ordered "one glass of orange juice to match the wall." I had just finished painting the kitchen wild tangerine.

As I set the juice in front of him, John impulsively leaned his head against my side, then squeezed me, his muscular arms around my waist. His affection had always been as spontaneous and impulsive as a child. When he released me I served him his coffee and scrambled eggs and bacon. Then I brought over my pot of tea, a cup and a saucer and slid in beside him.

"Look at the label on this tea bag," I said. "'Discontent breeds progress.' That describes me, John. I've been restless for months, but getting ready for this Florida trip has cured me."

John's face clouded. "The vacation is off, Bets. I just can't leave the station now."

He couldn't be serious, I thought to myself. I searched his face. It was sober and boyish, his pug nose dotted with freckles, but the amiable lightheartedness was gone. I had sensed a heaviness in him when he came home from work the previous night. Obviously not wanting a before-bedtime confrontation, he had waited until now to hand out the bad news.

"Why are you doing this to us?" I asked stonily.

"The new foreman isn't ready to handle things on his own and Ike's been gone for two days," he replied. "Our help situation is a mess."

"Ike is the problem," I snapped. "You've got to fire him. He only cares about two things—pork chops and Sweet Lucy (wine)." All my pent-up hostility toward black people poured out in those words.

"Ike is a good mechanic. I can't fire him just because he has a problem with Sweet Lucy," John replied evenly.

"Somewhere there must be another good mechanic you could hire," I said crossly.

John just shook his head. "It isn't only the problems at the station. We're loaded with debts and the vacation will only put us in deeper." He finished his breakfast quickly, gave me a peck on the cheek instead of the usual lingering kiss and charged out of the house. The zoom of the engine, and the grind of gears as he sped to work were just a few tell-tale signs of my husband's mad dash through life. "Jittery John" my mother called him. She would warn him that life was meant to be sipped, not gulped. John would just smile at her.

He was also inclined to think out loud. My parents, Glenn and Fern Perkins, had asked us to dinner several weeks before. While we were talking about our proposed Florida vacation at the table, John suddenly blurted out, "Come along with us. Dad, you can drive the boat while Betty and I water-ski. Brenda and Gary can play together, and Mother, think of the rest you will get under the warm Florida sun."

Although our two families got along very well, I wasn't certain that I wanted to spend a two-weeks' vacation with my parents. But as we talked my enthusiasm grew. Our daughter Brenda was six years old. My parents' last child, Gary, was also a six-year-old. When Mother and I were both obviously pregnant, we had embarrassed my brother Jim by sitting side by side wearing maternity dresses at his high school graduation. My baby was born first, so Mother took care of me and Brenda when I came out of the hospital. In return, five weeks later, I ministered to the needs of Mother and baby Gary. Not every mother can have a daughter and a brother so near the same age—who enjoy playing together as they grow up. Over the years Mother had become a kind of insurance policy during family get-togethers. She watched the children closely and was in constant prayer for the safety of all of us when we were around boats or traveling in the car.

As I washed the breakfast dishes and cleaned up the kitchen, I decided not to call my parents just yet with the news that John had cancelled our vacation. Perhaps he would change his mind again. I focused my thoughts on that probability. Prayer, to me, was the heart's desire put into words. "Lord, You know how much I want to go to Florida," I prayed softly.

There was more to this trip for me than just a Florida vacation. I was bored with our life in Terre Haute. Our comfortable ranch house, the convertible, the yellow and white cabin cruiser which we kept at nearby Lake Catarack—all things we had worked hard for—had somehow not brought us fulfillment. A change of location was needed, I had decided. And Florida had the answers for both John and me. A gasoline station in the travel-heavy vacation state would be ideal for my husband. With his drive, John could quickly develop it into an all-purpose automotive business, as he was doing in Terre Haute. For me, the year-round outdoor life would be a true answer to prayer. Expenses would be less too. No worry about winter coats and boots.

The morning's setbacks and irritations continued. Brenda awoke tired and cross; at the breakfast table she overturned a glass of milk. When I found a moment to relax and turned on the radio, the music that poured forth made me cringe. Oh no! It was Art Lindsey's program. The way this freelance preacher scrambled together country western music with religion was enough to ruin your day.

I suppose that part of my annoyance was caused by the way Art sauntered into our church on Sunday evenings and accompanied the song service with his guitar. We liked the way we had always handled this part of the program through organ music. Art was always putting the emphasis on praise.

"Let everyone that hath breath, praise the Lord," he would say, quoting Scripture. Then he would suggest songs that were folksy and not in keeping with the mood of the service.

I snapped off the radio and put on my favorite Jack Holcomb record; Holcomb's singing of the great old hymns fed me more than almost any sermon.

I went down the hall to make the beds and glanced with a pang at the matching mother and daughter swimsuits I had laid out to pack. They were yellow and white-checked gingham with a ruffle on the bottom of the short skirt; Brenda's had several rows of ruffles covering the seat section which she labeled her "bimer." The ruffle helped to hide my too-thin figure. I winced at the memory of myself at age thirteen standing five foot nine inches tall and weighing but 100 pounds. My brothers used to say, "We never believed that storks delivered babies until Betty was born. Most kids look like their parents, she looks like the stork." To offset my self-centeredness about my skinniness, I became an energetic doer, proud of my good health and school accomplishments in music, drama and academics. Learning that tall women rarely get sympathy because they never seem to appear as if they require it, I took pride in my independent attitude.

The thought spell was broken by the phone ringing. I wanted it to be John with good news—and it was. "Have you called your folks yet?" he began. "Good. This new man is working out fine and Ike is back on the job. The guys want me to take this vacation and they say they'll work extra hours if necessary. Let's take some money out of savings and leave tomorrow as planned. You need it; I need it. I can feel the tug of the tow rope, the spray in my face, and the sand between my toes already!"

His exuberant voice set my heart to singing. My dream was going to come true, all of it. There was only the faintest negative thought in the far reaches of my mind—a tiny inner premonition that I determinedly ignored.

The next morning, John and I were at the breakfast table when Brenda bounced through the door. "I'm all ready. I did my own packing," she announced proudly. She stood there with her long blonde curls, wide blue eyes and glowing pink cheeks. She was dressed in a blouse and ruffled panties, but no skirt. In her hand was a round pink plastic suitcase which she called her "suitbucket."

It's a good thing I decided to examine it. Out jumped her little black and white kitten "Pumpkin Face," named for his round countenance and entrance into the world on Halloween. Also tucked inside were her swimsuit, sunglasses, a red Delicious apple and four pieces of bubble gum.

"What will you sleep in?" I smiled at the absence of any night clothes.

"In our motel, of course, Mommie."

Dad and Mom and Gary arrived soon after breakfast. With careful planning we had decided that all six of us could fit fairly comfortably in our spacious Pontiac. Now came that frantic last-minute packing and closing up of the house. My dad put his car in our garage and began fitting luggage into the trunk of our convertible. Calm and unflappable at fifty, Dad's outspoken wisdom and unselfish strength fed both his family and the congregation of 300 he pastored thirty-one miles to the south. Dad loved the outdoors, whether it was hunting, fishing, boating or gardening. His gear always included a Bible, a concordance, and clipboard for making sermon notes.

In contrast, my forty-six-year-old mother, Fern Burns Perkins, was a worrier. A descendant of poet Robert Burns, she had inherited some of his gift for verse, but took her home-making role with total seriousness. Mother loved to bake and sew and keep an orderly house. During my school years I recall getting off the bus only twice when she wasn't there to meet me. Once she was in labor at the hospital having my third brother, Marvin; the other time she couldn't get home from shopping because a freight train was stuck for forty minutes at the crossing.

Her last son, Gary, taxed her patience to the limit. Adventuresome, with mischievous blue eyes, Gary had broken both arms in different escapades in the four-month period before our vacation trip. Once after a visit to the circus he tried unsuccessfully to tightrope-walk on the backyard clothes line. The other break came when he attempted an acrobatic flip over the round leather hassock in our living room. Arms now mended, he jumped out of the car, grabbed Brenda's hand and raced her to our backyard swing, an automobile tire hanging on a rope from the limb of our sycamore tree.

John was on the phone with last-minute instructions to his shop when I realized we had made no arrangements to have our family collie and kitten fed while we were gone. "You and your animals, Betty," was John's only comment when he heard my dilemma. Dogs and kittens had been a long tradition in our family. My grandmother, whom everyone called Mom Burns, told me once that my mother had twenty-two assorted animals at one period when she was a child.

I had just finished working out a plan for a neighbor to feed our animals when Mother came in the house, an exasperated look in her eyes. "Gary and Brenda have gotten filthy on that swing," she reported.

With one final flurry of energy on that warm June day in 1959, we closed and locked all the windows, turned off the water, left a note for the milkman, another note for the paperboy, said goodbye twice to the animals, brushed the dirt off Gary and Brenda, made three last-minute trips into the house to retrieve a jacket, a baseball glove and a piece of mosquito netting. I leaned back exhausted on the rear seat of the car as Dad drove out the driveway.

The adults may have been worn out, but the children certainly were not. Brenda, on my left, stood upon the floorboard behind the driver with her little arms wrapped around her grandfather's neck, tight enough to choke him. "This is my Papaw," she cried.

Uncle Gary, five weeks her junior, had been looking out the window on my right. Quickly he took exception. "This is no Papaw; this is my daddy," he shouted, pulling her away. Sitting between the two contestants, I began to wonder how much vacation there would be for us.

For John and I greatly needed it. My husband had worked day and night for months to make a success of his business. The vacation would help relax his frayed nerves. As for me, I was in a deep rut and desperately wanted a change. I felt I had been a good mother, wife, Sunday School teacher, church organist, and neighbor. Working so hard to make a good impression on others had deeply drained me. What was wrong? Why did there seem to be so little real joy in all my strivings and achievements?

For a moment I was envious of my father, who received such deep satisfactions from his faith. How did he do it? He went about things so calmly, almost effortlessly. Just the way he was driving now, relaxed, serene, at peace with himself and others. When prodded about his serenity, Dad would smile and say that all peace and power come from Jesus. The answer seemed so pat.

We ate dinner somewhere near Chattanooga, Tennessee, and decided not to stop for the night until we were well into the state of Georgia. John was driving and I was sitting in front with him and Brenda, who soon fell asleep against my side. As the car grew quiet I continued my musing. John could find a new business opportunity in Florida. It was such a logical move for an outdoor family. Our plans to build a new home in Terre Haute could be adjusted to the Florida terrain. Even Mother and Dad might want to move down and join us.

Brenda, as she slept, seemed a bit heavy leaning against my right side. I shifted her slightly, but the discomfort in my side remained. I shook it off and closed my eyes to dream about our future in Florida.

2

NIGHT EMERGENCY

CRYSTAL INN IS located twenty miles north of Clearwater, Florida—an unspoiled, lovely cypress lodge on the rim of the Gulf of Mexico and part of the Gulf Vista Retreat Center. The six of us were the only guests, taking over all the upstairs rooms where we could see the waves roll in. Our view was unhindered except for one spot in the center—an aged banyan tree, gnarled, with heavy waxed foliage, writhing in and out of the earth.

Much of our first vacation day was spent on the sunporch resting and listening to the rustling sound of palm fronds in the breeze and the lapping of the waves on the shore. The sand was the texture and color of fine white bleached cake flour; the water was crystal-clear.

The high point of the day was to see Brenda's face as she caught her first fish, just four and a half inches long, and pulled it out of the water. It was too small to eat, but she would not throw it back. She insisted she was going to take it to Indiana in the trunk of the car to show her other grandparents.

Gary had been entranced by the beach, too, especially the fiddler crabs. We spent an hour trying to teach him to float on his back in the water, but he had trouble relaxing. Irrepressible Gary never seemed to stop moving.

In many ways, my husband John and Gary were alike in their childlike approach to life. While my parents and I had been happy to relax on the sunporch and absorb the fragrances of Florida, John had been in and out of the water, up and down the beach on various investigative sorties, and then instigated a short trip to another island where we watched porpoises play and gathered up sand dollars along the shore.

One discordant episode occurred when John brought us the local afternoon newspaper. On the front page was a story about a young boy who had drowned nearby in the ocean. Mom sucked in her breath and vowed even closer supervision of Gary and Brenda. I found the story of this death a jarring and unpleasant note. It reminded me of my recent conversation with Dorothy Upchurch and her fears for John.

In the evening as the sun sank below the water, soft organ music began drifting out over the Gulf. It came from the steeple of an old church of Spanish structure, dull yellow stucco in color, nestled among tall stately palms at the end of Crystal Beach Avenue. Out on the water we could see fishermen in shrimp boats cut the motors of their boats to drift and listen. John was enjoying the music too, relaxed for the first time that day.

Amid the tranquility of the moment, my thoughts returned to the drowning we had read about that afternoon, and then to the only dead person I had ever seen—my tiny two-day-old baby brother.

"Mother, I'd like to ask you a question," I said suddenly. "How did you feel when your baby boy died so soon after his birth?"

My mother looked surprised at the unexpected question. "I grieved to be sure," she said softly, and we were silent for a while reliving that memory. The baby was a breech birth and his tiny spinal cord had snapped in the process. The private family service had been held in the beautiful chapel of a West Terre Haute funeral home. Age ten at the time, I sat next to Aunt Pearl in a lovely velvet chair, while my little brothers Don and Jim were with Mom Burns nearby. The tiny form lay in a small silvery blue casket banked with rosebuds and baby's breath flowers.

There had been organ music, and the pastor had read from Scripture and spoken a few words. At the close of the service I walked past the open casket and vividly remember how pretty he was—dark brown wavy hair, round face with olive skin. I did not grieve. I had not known him and felt no particular need for him since I already had two little brothers that I loved dearly.

"Grief can get to be very self-centered," Mother continued. "I soon realized that some day we would see our son in Heaven and that he would not have a severed spinal cord, but would be perfect and happy and so glad to see us. There would be a most joyful reunion."

"You make death sound like a such a happy event," I said, unconvinced.

"I believe that it is," Mother said while Dad nodded vigorously.

My doubts were obvious and I did not pursue the subject. Death was the end of life as I knew it. How could that be good news? John, too, was uncomfortable. If anything, he loathed the subject of death more than I did.

I snuggled up to my husband and reached for his hand. John's intensity had always attracted me. He had always reached out for life. It carried over into every area: work, play, love-making, and lately the church where he had begun energetically leading group-singing. In his early teens John and his two younger brothers had provided the main help for the family tomato farm in Middletown, Indiana. At fifteen John dreamed of owning a fancy car. By the time he had a driver's license he had worked so hard and saved so much he was able to buy a used Cadillac convertible and thus became the envy of his schoolmates.

Then came a period of youthful wildness which brought him close to death on two occasions. Once while driving a gravel truck at work, he overturned it on a slope and he and the truck tumbled into sixty-five feet of water. The water pressure made it impossible to open either the door or roll down the window. Somehow with his last breath he broke the window and swam to the surface.

One night while driving home after a drinking party, several boys in the car with him dared John to try and beat a train to the railroad crossing. Forgetting the freezing road conditions, John gunned the engine, hit an icy spot—and the car skidded into the moving train. John was the only one badly hurt, suffering a broken leg and bad cuts on his head and cheek.

I first met him one Sunday shortly after this mishap. He was on crutches and had beamed a lopsided grin in my direction, looking a bit comical with his bandaged head. I learned later that he had refused to go out with his crowd the night before, stating, "I'm going to church in the morning. I hear the new minister has a pretty daughter." They had just hooted at him.

That Sunday morning, he really did look as if he had been hit by a train. I saw a battered youth one inch smaller than me and was not a bit impressed, because I was looking for a tall sophisticated young man with polished charm and spiritual depth.

How grossly I underestimated John's drive and determination! He went home that Sunday and told his mother and dad that he was going to marry the preacher's daughter. John then left his wild crowd, entered into church activities and became a warmhearted, loving, and unselfish person, winning my heart in the process. We were married two years later at Thanksgiving.

John had been working in the heat treat department of a New Castle, Indiana, automobile assembly plant. His job was to take 90-pound axles and stick them into a blast furnace for tempering—a physically demanding task. Soon after our marriage, I persuaded him to move to Terre Haute where John became manager of the Sunoco service station at the corner of Ft. Harrison Road and Lafayette Avenue. Johnny's Sunoco Corner soon expanded to eight pumps, a car wash, a tire and battery business, and then a used car lot. Always the materialistic dreamer, I foresaw a series of service stations for John, who would then move into an executive role.

Despite his drive John had an impractical side, such as his disconcerting habit of giving credit to poor risks. Poverty-stricken travelers from the south (Kentucky hillbillies) coming north on Highway 41 to Chicago looking for work would stop and were soon telling John their hard-luck stories. My husband would often refuse to take their money, insisting they pay him by mail when they found work. Sometimes they sent the money, sometimes not. I recall one bearded little man who sent us a dollar a week for almost a year to pay for a set of tires.

There were times when John's generous nature made me want to hug him—such as when he would take out his own handkerchief to wipe a child's runny nose, or gently steer a youngster into the washroom, or give a free soda to some tired and impoverished traveler. Then there were occasions when his tenderheartedness made me want to throw a bucket of water on him, like that hectic day before Christmas one year when he arrived home in the middle of the day with a carful of children. I was supposed to babysit while their weary parents went shopping for presents.

My biggest problem after our marriage had been with his mother. I sensed Mother Upchurch's disapproval of me from the start and was always on the defensive. John was mostly unaware of the tension that grew between the two women he loved the most. Like his father, Oscar Upchurch, he was easygoing and avoided family confrontations. This came out especially over the issue of which church we should attend.

John had always gone to his family church where the service was dignified and carefully structured. In my denomination there was more freedom of worship and lively singing, sometimes with guitars. After our marriage John became paralyzed with indecision, not wanting to displease either his mother or me. Although a bit disdainful of other churches, I would have gone to his if he had asked me, but for seven months he would not go to church at all. Then one Sunday morning, without a word, he dressed in his best suit and accompanied me to our church. Later he joined.

My resentment of my mother-in-law often came out in the "pity parties" which the wives of her two other sons occasionally held with me when our husbands were at work. I think deep down we both respected and feared her, but it certainly was not easy to love Mother Upchurch.

Somewhat guiltily I reflected on the way I had distorted the story of John's and my honeymoon trip. Since John could not afford to take me on a honeymoon when we were married, his mother and sister Helen volunteered to accompany us to

Niagara Falls. Mrs. Upchurch agreed to pay all the expenses, but I never told that part of the story, nor that John and I drove alone to Niagara Falls while his mother and sister stayed for a visit with a relative in Port Allegheny, Pennsylvania. I had always put the emphasis on the meddlesome mother-in-law angle and cast Mother Upchurch in the role of the heavy as I told how she accompanied us on our honeymoon.

Uneasily I recalled how during her last visit only a few days before Dorothy Upchurch had sensed my restlessness and chided me about it in her incisive manner.

"You must learn to be satisfied with what you have, young lady. It's there in the Bible. Philippians 4:11. *I have learned, in whatever state I am, to be content.* And for you and me that should mean the state of Indiana too," she concluded with surety.

I had stared at her in dismay, wondering how she had so accurately understood my state of mind. And her quote from Philippians was on target. The material things in life often pulled me away from spiritual matters, but for some reason Scripture always spoke to me—and had from the time of my conversion at age thirteen.

Still tired from the long trip from Indiana and groggy from the hot sun, we all returned early. John was instantly asleep while I lay in bed fighting a nagging pain in my side that had begun after dinner. I eased out of bed and went out on the screened balcony, watching the beacon on the lighthouse at the tip of a nearby island. The pain in my side throbbed with each blink. Finally, I went back inside, awoke John and told him I needed a doctor. He was instantly alarmed and roused my parents. Dad and John quickly helped me to the car, leaving Mother with the sleeping children. We decided to head for the small beach hospital at Tarpon Springs, nine miles away, which we had passed on the highway.

As we drove out of Crystal Beach the waving fronds on the Robolina and Saga date palms had lost their lustre. The gnarled old banyan tree reminded me of a stooped old witch. For I was writhing with so much nausea that I wondered when I would have to ask my dad to stop and let me be sick by the side of the road. In a matter of minutes we pulled up in front of the hospital.

The Tarpon Springs Hospital seemed smaller even than the veterinarian clinic at home. A male attendant quickly approached the car door with a wheelchair. I stepped out and was about to reject it when a wave of weakness made me sink into it gratefully.

Inside, the attendant steered me to the emergency room and helped me onto the examining table. I clenched my fists, determined to be stoical, remembering the many times in my childhood when my anemic and usually pregnant mother would be stretched out on the couch in a faint. It always seemed to happen with many members of the family present, and assorted grandmothers and aunts would bend over her with cold cloths for her forehead and rub her wrists to stimulate circulation. Mixed with my love and concern was the suspicion that she somehow enjoyed her misery. As I grew older I was determined never to show this kind of weakness.

Dr. James Thompson, the night doctor on duty, was young and gentle. I decided he was too young and good-looking to be wise. As he applied pressure to my lower right side, the ceiling lights separated into small bright specks, like lighted fish eggs, and I passed out. So much for my vow to be strong and unflinching.

When my eyes began to focus again, the doctor asked a series of questions, then did a urinalysis, a blood test and X-rays. After checking results, he spoke frankly.

"You're in trouble. I'm in trouble. I'm afraid that you have a swollen appendix, ready to burst. The blood test shows an infection. I have only twenty-four beds in this little beach hospital and I have twenty-six patients, two of whom are women in labor. I am the only doctor on duty. Your appendix must be removed immediately, but I cannot do it here."

A hurried call was made to the Morton Plant Hospital in Clearwater, Florida, and arrangements completed for the head surgeon on the staff of that hospital to meet me there and have the operating room ready. Dr. Thompson warned me: "If you get relief, you'll know your appendix has ruptured. Do not be persuaded otherwise. Go through with the operation. You need surgery immediately."

The doctor then gave me a shot to ease the pain. Minutes later the throbbing eased and I felt a kind of euphoria. Everything was going to work out fine, I concluded.

Two ambulance attendants entered the emergency room and began preparing me carefully for the twenty-two-mile ride to the Clearwater hospital. They wrapped the white sheet about me as neatly mitred at the corners as a bride's gift for a wedding shower. Then I was lifted gently and seemed to float into the back of the ambulance, the interior of which was quilted and carpeted, with velvet draperies lining the windows. John sat beside me holding my hand, while Dad drove our car behind the ambulance.

I was still euphoric and yet aware of everything—the rotating red light reflecting through the windows, the screaming siren muted somewhat by the well-insulated interior of the vehicle. We were quiet and very much alone, as the drivers had closed the curtain behind them. John then began philosophizing and continued to do so during the rest of the ride to Clearwater.

"How silly our value system is," he began. "We think that money and what we own are so important until a time like this. So last month Sunoco gave me the 'salesman of the month' award; it seemed so important then, but what good is it now? My mother is right—she told me that if you have the Lord and your health, that's all a marriage really needs. It seemed so simplistic, but she's right, Bets."

A male attendant, a nurse's aide and a registered nurse met us at the emergency entrance of the Clearwater Hospital and wheeled me into the prep room adjoining surgery. The necessary papers were filled out and my side was shaved and painted. Dr. Malcolm White, an older man with a harried look, began to examine me. Finally he removed his glasses, wiped his face with his handkerchief, and with a reassuring smile said, "I'm glad Dr. Thompson was not able to operate on you in his hospital. With all due respect to another doctor, I feel he has made a wrong analysis. It would have unnecessarily ruined a vacation for your two families. You have an internal infection which I think we can clear up with penicillin. We'll keep you here for a day or so until the infection is gone and the dizziness subsides. You'll be as good as new!"

This was what we wanted to hear. John and Dad returned to our vacation lodge and I went to sleep, reassured.

But the infection did not clear up. Day after day, the doctors conferred, ran tests, and gave me shots of penicillin for the infection. The pain returned. When my temperature began to climb, they called in another specialist in internal medicine. After studying the X-rays, he said, "I feel you may have a tubular pregnancy."

On the seventh day of my stay in the Clearwater Hospital several of the doctors gathered together in my room for an "organ recital"—a review, it seemed, of every part of my lower anatomy. When I protested this, John and my dad intervened to suggest that I be flown back to Indiana and admitted to our local hospital there. The doctors agreed to release me, and hours later I was on a plane with John and Brenda for Terre Haute.

When the plane landed at the Terre Haute airport, I asked John to take me home. He was surprised.

"I thought the doctors told you to check into the hospital as soon as you arrived," he said.

"John, the doctors can't agree on anything about me. Dr. Thompson said one thing, Dr. White something else. They've discussed me endlessly, pawed over me day after day. I'm tired of the whole thing. Let's go home. I'll find a way to clear up the infection." Then I remembered that my parents and Gary were driving back in our car from Florida. "I'll be admitted to the hospital when Mom and Dad get home," I said.

Reluctantly John agreed, on the promise that I would go to bed. He didn't have to pressure me. I felt terrible. But I had another problem too. In my head. It was pride.

As I look back on that decision, it was completely indefensible. Why did I deliberately disobey the doctor's instructions to enter myself into the hospital? The reason I gave John about the doctors not being able to agree on what was wrong with me was true enough. Yet that didn't get to the real issue.

I realize now that I have always been a person who liked to run things. A fierce dislike of hospitals was being born in me because there I found myself utterly out of control. The patient lies on the high bed like a horizontal department store dummy, made to feel like a thing—a piece of anatomy with problem parts—not like a person at all. Was it false modesty or prudishness that made me shrink from the casual uncovering for breast or vaginal or rectal examinations, the constant chatter about my female trouble at the Clearwater Hospital?

Then too one is always at the mercy of the hospital routine—stick the thermometer in the mouth at 6:00 a.m. . . . wake the patient out of a good sleep . . . slap a washcloth on her face fifteen minutes later . . . leave her sitting on the bedpan for twenty minutes—there is little the patient can do to alter the course of events.

Complaining did little good, I found, and often resulted in poor service and less attention. Trying to talk to the doctors did not help much either. I could see it in their eyes and in their impatience always to be off—*I have the knowledge . . . she has none . . . let her talk a little . . . be kind. . . .*

I kept thinking, "But it's *my* body you doctors are discussing. It's *my* life and *my* future at stake. How can you bypass *me* this way?" As a person I felt kicked into the corner and ignored. So I found the whole hospital system an assault on my personhood.

Oh, I tried to be bright and cheery. I would greet the nurses with warmth and the doctors with open friendliness. I wanted them to think me a good patient. But underneath I was in rebellion, primarily because of a feeling of helplessness. I didn't know then how to handle that.

So by trying to take things in my own hands and refusing to enter the hospital for further treatment, I put myself on a collision course between two forces—my pride and a deadly infection.

3

THE COMFORTER

THREE DAYS LATER I awoke in a panic. I was afire with fever. My body had swelled up like a blimp. I could not move my legs, had no feeling in my hands and could barely get my breath.

"John, wake up, wake up. I'm in trouble." The voice hardly sounded like me. It seemed to be coming from across the room. Then I became almost hysterical when I realized I could not see.

John bounded from bed and dialed my parents. "Pray for Bets; she's much worse. Meet us at the hospital emergency room as soon as you can get there."

Then he was calling the hospital, asking for a surgeon. "This is an emergency!" John said, his voice cracking.

I faded and returned, faded and returned again. Feeling came into my hands; they had been asleep. Vision in my eyes returned slightly, but I could not smell or taste.

John dialed a neighbor who agreed to come right over and stay with Brenda. He dressed quickly, then found a bathrobe for me. I felt his arms under my knees and shoulders just as Brenda came into the room.

I focused my eyes enough to see my daughter standing in the doorway in her pajamas with the pink teddy bears printed on them. Under one arm was "Jingles," her large stuffed donkey; in the other was "Pete," her life-sized stuffed monkey.

"What's wrong with Mommie? She's big enough to walk, Daddy; why are you carrying Mommie?"

"It's all right, dear," I said groggily.

As John carried me to the car, I blacked out. A few minutes later I came to when John sped around a corner, tires squealing. As we pulled up in front of the emergency entrance of Union Hospital, a stream of thoughts seared my consciousness like a lightning bolt. I had been born at this hospital; now I was returning here to die.

The next thing I recall was opening my eyes to blurred lights on the ceiling of the examining room, swirling about like a lake of tiny minnows. A physician was standing over me. My husband, remembering that the last examination in the Florida hospital indicated a possible tubular pregnancy and a dead fetus, had called Dr. Paul Bherne, who was a gynecologist and surgeon.

As I faded in and out of my twilight zone, I recall Dr. Bherne sitting at the right corner of the examining cot, taking a ball-point pen from his pocket and scrawling on the white bed sheet a diagram for my husband. He drew a picture of the womb, the tubes and ovaries. "Her tubular pregnancy took place here," he said, pointing to the right tube. "The fetus has been dead for some time: this explains the gangrenous infection in your wife's bloodstream."

Before I was wheeled to the operating room, I was asked to sign several papers releasing the hospital of responsibility if anything went wrong during surgery. Because of my blurred vision these were read to me and a nurse helped me sign in the proper place. One of the papers, a copy of which I retained, was titled: "Consent to Operation that Will Result in Sterilization."

> I, the undersigned, a patient in Union Hospital, Terre Haute, Indiana, hereby certify: That I have full knowledge that the nature of the operation to be performed under the direction of Dr. Paul Bherne will result in sterilization; that consent thereto is hereby given voluntarily by me, if competent, and for me by my parents, guardian or best friend, as the case may be, if incompetent for any reason; that the Union Hospital and Dr. Bherne shall in no way be held liable for the resulting sterilization.

Below my signature there was another statement for John to sign:

> I, the spouse of Betty Upchurch, the patient above-mentioned, and knowing the contents and meaning of the above instrument, fully agree, request, consent and advise that said operation be performed.

We were signing away any possibility of adding to our family; yet what choice did we have? How sad that Brenda would never have a brother or sister!

I was rolled to the operating room and placed on the table. Another doctor and an anesthetist joined Dr. Bherne. They gave me a spinal injection, then a shot of sodium pentathol in the right arm, and then the countdown—99, 98, 97. I heard myself complaining that it was too cold on that operating table, that he was cutting me too deep, clear through my back and into the table. Dr. Bherne, speaking to a nurse, said, "I know she can't possibly feel that. More sodium pentathol, please."

I didn't feel anything from then on, but pieces of conversation from the medical men pierced my befogged senses. There were comments about "a huge mass," many technical terms, then before I slipped into deep unconsciousness the words, "I don't see how she can survive this massive gangrenous infection."

In my childhood our family used to hold yearly family picnics outside of Rockville, Indiana, beside the brown, one-lane, 30-foot covered bridge which spanned the Wasbash River. The river, although swift-moving through this wooded area, was wide enough and deep enough for swimming. The water was so fresh and pure that we drank it.

My uncles loved to roughhouse with us children at these picnics, particularly Uncle Jesse, whose position as a railroad brakeman earned my deep admiration. Uncle Jesse would pick up like a sack of potatoes. Then I would squeal with delight as I sailed through the air from one uncle's strong arms to another.

In the recovery room after the operation, as my temperature soared to 105 degrees and the morphine took full effect, I dreamed that once again I was flying through the air from uncle to uncle. Then suddenly the scene changed from the Wabash River to a large city, and some tiny pink men were tossing me from a church steeple to the top of an apartment house to a skyscraper. The dwarfed creatures would scream with laughter each time I would almost fall to the ground. Next I found myself being hurled from one jet plane to another as planes were whizzing about me in all directions. There was a terrible pain in my stomach which got worse each time one of the small creatures touched me.

44

Was this death, I wondered? The voice in the operating room had said I could not survive the infection, yet how could this be death if I could feel such pain? Then I rallied to sound—it was the voice of Dr. Bherne.

"I have never cut into such a nasty mess in all my eighteen years of practice."

Then I heard my father's voice, but not what he said. Then it was Dr. Bherne talking again:

"Dr. Thompson was right in his diagnosis. There was no tubular pregnancy. It was a ruptured appendix. Why, her appendix burst with such impact that all I found of it were small fragments. I didn't even attempt to remove them. Nor did I try to suture the incision back together again. We will leave it open to drain."

As they talked on I only half heard the words, but my father later gave me the substance of Dr. Bherne's grim prognosis for me. Peritonitis infection had coated all my organs, causing some to disintegrate. "I have seen 200-pound men die with a ruptured appendix and no complications," he told my parents. "Your daughter has carried that mass of infection for eleven days. I'm sure it's now spread all through her body. She's a desperately sick woman."

Since few hospitals had intensive-care units in 1959, arrangements were made for around-the-clock nursing—three nurses a day, eight hours each. A stomach pump, connected by a long tube through my nose, had to be closely monitored so that it was properly irrigated and would thus prevent vomiting and hemorrhaging. My blood pressure, pulse and heartbeat were constantly checked. Dr. Bherne asked my parents to keep an eye on the intravenous feeding process to see that the needle connection into the vein during blood transfusions was kept secure. My veins had not responded fully because of the high fever and high infectious content of my blood.

Close relatives could visit me, the doctor said, one or two at a time. Either of my parents or John could remain day and night by my side without restrictions.

I knew that this was an extremely difficult time for John. Hospitals and doctors had always intimidated him. Death was something he would just never talk about. Dad told me later that the sight of my drawn white face after the operation had paralyzed him with fear. For days afterward he would arrive for a visit, pat me softly on the shoulder and then station himself outside, seated on the floor and leaning against the door in an attempt to protect me from visitors. He would sit there for hours at a time, moving only to let nurses, doctors and members of the family enter and leave.

I wanted to comfort John, but was too weak. When he would enter the room and kiss me lightly on the cheek, I could barely open my eyes. I needed him there beside me to tell me his business troubles and report on Brenda. It seemed that everyone decided that because my eyes were closed most of the time, I could neither hear nor see what was going on in the room. In reality, I was intensely aware of what was going on.

While Mother stayed home with Brenda and Gary, Dad Perkins would sit by my bed day and night. At certain periods he would stand beside me and pray. Oh, how I remember those prayers! The words were like living water dripping into my veins, a healing balm for a fever-ridden spirit. Dad's prayers were so real, so true, so powerful that they were better than any life-support system. He said things like:

"Lord, we are so weak, but You are strong. How we love You, how we trust You, how completely and totally we depend on You. Betty is Your child, Lord Jesus, and she needs Your love and Your tenderness and Your compassion and Your healing touch. We do not beg for her life for any selfish reason of our own. You loaned her to us for a few years and yet we know she has always belonged to You. Oh, how we praise You for Your goodness to us during these years, for the blessings You poured upon us, for Your day-by-day presence in our home. We can sense Your love filling this room now. Thank You, Lord Jesus, for Your comforting Presence."

As the words of my father's prayer sank into my mind, I was suddenly convicted of something. Jesus was very real to Dad. Was He to me? For years I had prayed to Him, sung to Him, quoted Him, but I had to admit that I did not feel close to Jesus.

The fault was obviously mine. I had become too involved with my worldly life and felt no need for Him. Up until now I had never really been sick. My parents and John had provided comfort. Brenda had given me fulfillment as a mother. When on earth, Jesus had responded to the needs of people. Up to this point I had had no needs.

A series of scenes flashed before me. I was thirteen. It was Sunday night and Dad had preached a moving sermon on our need to accept Jesus Christ as Savior. We were to be ready for His Second Coming. No one wanted to be left out of the marvelous life which He promised us in eternity.

We drove home from church that evening through northeast Terre Haute, not far from the Paul Cox airfield. From the window of the car I saw a light in the sky descending toward that small airport. Remembering my father's sermon, I wondered, "Could that be Jesus coming back? Was I ready for Him?"

It was a plane coming in for a landing, but my mind remained stimulated. Later, lying in bed in the darkness of my room that night so many years ago, I found myself repeating the words of a prayer I had stopped saying years before:

> Now I lay me down to sleep;
> I pray the Lord my soul to keep.
> If I should die before I wake,
> I pray the Lord my soul to take.

The third line then began to bother me: "If I should die before I wake. . . ." Could this happen? If so, would I miss out on all that the Bible promised? "I'm not ready to die," I thought to myself.

I jumped out of bed and went to my parents' bedroom door. Their light was out. I knocked anyway. "What is it?" my father asked sleepily.

I was embarrassed, then blurted out the first words that came to mind: "I'm not ready to die."

Instantly both parents were wide awake. In his sensitive spirit, Dad knew exactly what to do. He took me by the hand and he and Mom led me down to the living room.

"Betty, are you ready to commit your life to the Lord Jesus?" I nodded.

I knelt between my mother and father in front of our three-cushioned brown floral couch, one hand in Dad's, the other in Mother's. "Lord, I accept You as my personal Savior. I surrender my life to You for You to do with it what You will."

Then Dad read me some passages in Scripture where Jesus is talking to Martha just before He raises Lazarus from the dead: "Jesus said to her, *I am the resurrection and the life; he who believes in me, though he die, yet shall he live, and whoever lives and believes in me shall never die*" (John 11:25, 26).

Thirteen years had passed since that night, during which I had gone to church faithfully and tried to live virtuously. But there in my hospital bed I felt His gentle correction: I had lived by rules, but I did not know Jesus. Therefore I had missed the most important part of the Christian life.

Despite the fever and pain, I was aware of the beginning of a teaching process in my spirit. Something in me had been activated by Dad's prayers; my spirit and God's Spirit were touching. Then a strange thing happened.

For years I had loved the recordings of Jack Holcomb, two in particular: "The Old Account Was Settled Long Ago" and "I Have Been Born Again." While lying so helpless in my hospital bed, I heard the music of these great old hymns and the unforgettable words of the latter:

> My heart glows with rapture,
> My cup runneth o'er,
> Such joy, so transporting,
> I ne'er knew before;
> It flows thro' my soul from God's heavenly store,
> For I have been born again.
>
> I'll sing it, and tell it wherever I go,
> I want all to hear it,
> I want all to know,
> The joy of salvation
> That makes the heart glow,
> For I have been born again.

During one period of consciousness, I thanked the nurse for giving me this wonderful background music. She looked at me suspiciously and said there was no music in hospital rooms. How then had I heard it so clearly?

Then two events took place which made me more aware than ever before that the Comforter was with me. The first involved the visit of my mother-in-law.

Mother Upchurch had driven from New Castle, Indiana, some 150 miles across the state. The first time she walked into the hospital room with John, negative vibrations began to flow between us. My eyes were closed, but I could almost see her dark snapping eyes studying me, the life support equipment, the vases of flowers. She clucked sympathetically over me for a few minutes, then seeing that I could not respond, turned her attention to John. The questions began.

Was Brenda receiving good care? Who was looking after the house? Were you eating properly? And getting enough sleep? As the interrogation between mother and son continued I learned that John had been living alone in the house (Brenda was at my parents') and that the kitchen had been full of dirty dishes. John admitted ruefully that he had hired a young girl at a dollar an hour to wash the dishes. It had taken her six hours to do them.

I found myself getting upset at my mother-in-law's concern for John. I was the one near death, not John. It was almost as if the whole situation were my fault and she, Dorothy Upchurch, had to get things back in proper order, which she obviously intended to do, beginning with my kitchen.

Yet as I felt my resentment rising the way it always had when I encountered John's mother, a surprising thing happened. Something cool poured over my agitated spirit to quiet me. Like a refreshing ointment soothes bruised skin, this coolness extinguished the hot feelings within me. Then the words were implanted in my mind: *She has reason to worry about John; but she also loves you and someday you will see her as I do and love her too.*

Then it was as if a section of Scripture moved onto a screen in front of my eyes. The verses seemed to be a part of a long psalm:

> The earth, O Lord, is full of thy steadfast love;
> Teach me thy statutes!
> Thou hast dealt well with thy servant, O Lord,
> According to thy word.
> Teach me good judgment and knowledge,
> For I believe in thy commandments.
> Before I was afflicted I went astray. . . .
>
> (Psalm 119:64–67)

The words of the last verse seemed to enlarge until it stood out from the others. I began to tremble. *Before I was afflicted I went astray.* The Holy Spirit was showing me something through God's Word: that I had gone astray, that I had many things to make right and not just with my mother-in-law. Then I heard the gentle words: *Those who suffer for Me can minister for Me.*

My second experience of the Presence took place at the end of three tortuous days caused by a blockage in my bowel. Before taking me back to surgery, the doctors decided to relieve my distress with a manual procedure that is acutely uncomfortable and embarrassing. As two nurses with rubber gloves worked on me, I gritted my teeth and thought to myself, "This is the most humiliating experience of my life." And as I reached out for the Comforter, a wonderful change took place inside me.

My pride began to slip away as if I were shedding a frayed old skirt. I forgot that I had a body of different parts, some to be seen, some to be concealed. I became one body, one person, one spirit. And as I reached out for Jesus, He laid His hand on my head with such tenderness that I knew He was seeing me as I really was in the world of Spirit. The pain and discomfort fused into a moment of pure ecstasy.

And then there was a quick vision of how God had originally meant us all to be at our creation. Adam and Eve in the Garden of Eden—happy, carefree, unaware of any knowledge of good and evil, unaware of the need for concealment of anything about their personhood, free and open to God and each other.

At the same time I felt a sudden infilling of my body with what I can only describe as a torrent of love. It was the love of Jesus for me, ministered through two compassionate women. In turn, I had the intense and overwhelming desire to love

Christ with all my heart, as well as all of His ministering angels. This joy and love so flooded me that I thought I might burst.

There followed a period of sudden relief from pain as though Jesus were saying, "You see now—you can depend upon me to be with you in your moments of agony and despair."

This was exactly the kind of reassurance I needed to face the days that lay ahead.

4

CAPTIVE LISTENER

TWO DAYS LATER I was wheeled back into the operating room for more surgery. X-rays now showed that the ruptured appendix had caused a telescoping of the bowel and thus a blockage. As during the first operation, doctors and nurses assumed that since I was under anesthesia, I could hear nothing of what was said. And so they spoke quite negatively about my chances for recovery.

I have since learned that other patients have had this same experience. A friend of mine named Ida told me that she had been desperately sick in the hospital several years ago. Thinking her completely unconscious, her two children, a son and a daughter, began arguing over who would get certain items of her estate. It was such an ugly scene that Ida, who heard it all, was spurred on to recovery. "I fooled them two ways," she laughingly told me. "I lived, and then changed my will, leaving everything to my niece."

Even when under deep anesthesia, spoken words seem to be received by the patient's unconscious mind, collected and transferred to the brain in a process little understood. There can be a time lapse of hours, even days, before this translation process occurs and the patient has an awareness of what was said. After both operations I knew by their comments that my doctors considered me a hopeless case. I even recall the jokes about my Florida tan.

The result was a struggle inside me between two forces—a feeling of defeat which said that I might as well give up, and a fighting determination not to quit but to battle back. I resisted defeat, but I can see how some people might not. And I wonder how many unexplainable sudden post-operative deaths have resulted from patients who heard their death warrants under anesthesia, and in a state of despair gave up and died.

The problem of negative influences continued in my room for days after the operation. Only family members were allowed to visit me, but I belong to a large family. I've since spent hours reflecting on conversations I heard while seemingly unconscious; I've made notes and pondered the whole subject of how the vibrations, attitudes and dialogue of visitors can poison the atmosphere in a hospital room—or bless it.

Three women dropped in for a visit several days or so after my first operation. I later put down on paper the type of things they said:

"Betty's so young too. I believe twenty-seven."

"That's about the age of Susan. She left a four-year-old girl."

"What happened?"

"Susan was riding the ferris wheel at the circus over in Marshall, Illinois. She fell out. Broke her neck."

"How awful! Had she been drinking?"

"We think so. She and Sam were having problems. Sam's remarried now."

"It didn't take him long."

"Brenda will take Betty's death so hard. She and her mother are very close."

"I don't think John will marry anyone who would mistreat Brenda."

"The husband never knows. He's gone too much. John is at his shop day and night."

At this point I was relieved when the subject was changed to operations; but only for a while.

"I hear that it was a doctor in Florida who messed up Betty's case. He diagnosed it as some kind of malformed pregnancy."

"I would think there would be tests to tell the difference between a pregnancy and appendicitis."

"You would certainly think so."

"If, by some miracle, Betty recovers, she should sue."

"It probably wouldn't do any good."

"I guess not. There was the woman in New Goshen who was sewed up after an operation with a sponge still inside her. She had to go back to the hospital for another operation to get it removed. Some tiny veins started to grow through the sponge."

The women chatted on and on as though they were at a coffee klatsch in one of their homes. When they got up to leave, they stopped a minute by my bed. I'll never forget the brief prayer one said: "Lord, give her a peaceful hour in which to pass."

Another woman came to pray for me. Valerie was from our church and I had worked with her on special youth programs. She stood by my bed and began to weep.

"Lord, we want Your will for Betty," she began. Then her voice took on a sepulchral tone. "We all have to die sometime, Lord, and we want to be prepared. We pray that You will spare

Betty and let her remain with us. But our life here is so short and Your eternity is so long, so we know it is never right to ask for special favors. Instead, we want to be so totally in Your will that whether we live or die makes no difference . . ."

Valerie's heart was loving and her intention utterly self-less. What she said may have been true enough, but the tone of her voice and her weeping mannerisms told me she believed I was going to die. This left me depressed.

Then there was the young couple who came to see me one evening when I was alone. They stood quietly by the bed for a few moments. I was aware of their presence but did not open my eyes. They sat down and began to talk to each other. The husband began:

"Marge, you've left the newspaper in the driveway for two days now. I've told you about this before. It gives the impression we are away and invites prowlers."

"Well, let's stop the delivery. You can pick up the paper on the way home from the office."

"No. That won't work. Some days I'm not near the newsstand."

"Well, you're as bad as I am. When I drove the kids to camp, I came back to find the mail left in the box for two days. One envelope had come open through the humidity and there was seven dollars in cash inside."

"Marge, I had to be gone part of that time on a trip with George."

"I hear he and his wife are getting a divorce."

"It looks that way. Emily's drinking is driving him up the wall."

"I hear that George is chasing around."

There was a short silence.

"I don't think those rumors are fair to George. He has taken a lot in that marriage." Then followed a quick change of subject. "Let's not stay here long. We've got to stop for gas. I'm on empty now, and I want to work some on the lawn."

"By the way," said Marge, "there was a warning on television that we should not water the lawn. The drought seems to be worse. All of Indiana, Illinois, and Ohio are in trouble."

"That's all we need. No water."

The couple got up to leave and I was anguished on the inside. With my high fever I had been craving a drink of water, but because of the stomach pump connected by tube through my nose, I was not allowed any liquids in my mouth. Instead, a nurse would rub ice on my lips. Thus the news of a water shortage suddenly depressed me. Though grateful that they had cared enough to stop by, once again my spirit was disturbed. I was left with the feeling that people had written me off as so hopelessly ill that what they said did not matter.

My father was my anchor during those critical first days of high temperature and unconsciousness. For one stretch of eight days he hardly took time to change clothes as he sat with me day and night. In addition to his prayers, there was one phrase he often used which held me fast to the mooring. He would stand by my bed, touch my hand or arm or place his hand on my forehead and say softly, "Bless the name of Jesus."

The words drifted through my fog of pain and fever like soothing crystals of light, dissolving in my body with a deep healing effect. I had played hundreds of hymns on the organ extolling the name of Jesus, but I never knew the full power in His name until that moment. It was as though Jesus Himself was somehow spreading through my tissues, cleansing the poison, nourishing my blood, strengthening muscles and tendons and protecting the life system of veins and arteries. How I loved to hear my father repeat that phrase: "Bless the name of Jesus."

John was in and out during those days and I could sense his worry and tension. His body could hardly remain still.

He could not sit in a chair. My inert form and closed eyes unnerved him. I kept wanting to say, "John, I love you. Relax, just hold my hand and talk to me. I can hear you. I just don't want to open my eyes. Don't be fearful."

When John did try to pray, his words were hesitant as though to ask God to heal me might bring him a disappointment. I caught the same cautious tone from preachers as well as lay people. They were praying, "We ask that Your will be done with this desperately sick woman." I understand the reluctance some people have to pray with all-out faith. From the viewpoint of having been a very sick woman, hedged prayers almost made me feel that God was a capricious Father who couldn't be trusted to do the right thing by His children.

My mother had to care for our six-year-old during the first days after the operation. When she walked into my hospital room for the first time, she looked at my greenish face, gasped and slumped to the floor. A nurse was summoned while Daddy lifted her into a chair and began rubbing her wrists. She revived quickly but spent the rest of her visit talking in a whisper as though afraid to waken me. I wanted to comfort Mother somehow. "I know I must look awful, Mother, but I'm aware of what is going on. Please don't whisper. I want to hear what you're saying. And don't be so melodramatic. Just tell me about Brenda and Gary."

It was almost as if Mother heard me. The next time she visited my room accompanied by her older sister, my Aunt Lillian, she was much more positive. While making a tour of the flowers that had been sent by relatives and friends, she directed her conversation to me.

"Betty, you may not hear me," Mother said, "but I think I'll read you these get-well cards and describe the flower arrangements." She did so with help from her sister.

Then Aunt Lillian, who was the principal of the Marion Heights Elementary School in northwest Terre Haute, spoke of a visit she had had with Brenda.

"Brenda can't understand why she isn't allowed to visit you, Bets. She says she doesn't have any germs that would hurt you. Meanwhile, she's been visiting her daddy at work and asked for the job of cleaning the windshield of every car that stops for gas. She says she wants to earn money to help pay your hospital bill.

"Gary wants you to know that he was out to the lake Saturday and has learned to float on his back. And he has taught Brenda to ride the two-wheeler bike. Your mother is so good with them, Bets."

On they went, chatting about family news as though I were wide awake and alert. How I loved it! When they got up to leave and stood by my bed, I tried to open my eyes. All they did was flutter. But the two women noticed and got excited.

"I believe Betty does know we're here," Mother said. Each kissed me tenderly. My spirit was so refreshed by their visit.

Aunt Gertrude was another who knew exactly how to handle herself when she visited me. She would stride into the room, pick up my hand and hold it gently but firmly. "Keep your chin up, Bets. You'll be home with your family soon. And just remember this, too—we need you back playing the organ at our church."

Each time the words were different, but there was always a life line thrown to me with a ringing affirmation that I would soon get back into the action. And I began to believe I would.

One day I heard the footsteps of a man entering my room and at first assumed they belonged to either my husband or my father. The steps stopped at the foot of my bed. I heard the pages of a book being turned. When he started to read, I recognized the voice of Art Lindsey—the man who had annoyed me so much with his radio program of sermonettes and country music:

> Oh give thanks to the Lord,
>   for he is good;
> for his steadfast love endures
>   forever!

At first I was so conscious of the man I didn't hear the words. "Why is he here?" I asked myself. "Doesn't he know how sick I am? Only close relatives should come in here."

> Some wandered in desert wastes,
> Finding no way to a city to
>   dwell in;
> hungry and thirsty,
>   their soul fainteth within them.
> Then they cried to the Lord in
>   their trouble,
> and he delivered them from
> their distress. . . .

As Art read on I calmed down and listened to the words:

> Some were sick through their
>   sinful ways,
> And because of their iniquities
>   suffered affliction;
> They loathed any kind of food,
>   and they drew near to the gates
>   of death.
> Then they cried to the Lord in
>   their trouble,
> And he delivered them from
>   their distress;
> He sent forth his word, and
>   healed them,

And delivered them from destruction.
Let them thank the Lord for his
    steadfast love,
For his wonderful works to the
    sons of men!
And let them offer sacrifices of
    thanksgiving,
And tell of his deeds in songs
    of joy!

(Psalm 107:1, 4–6, 17–22)

The words ended like a benediction, filling my soul with hope. How gentle and loving and dedicated was this man! As he walked from the room, I knew that Art Lindsey was indeed God's messenger of good news. I knew too that God had used Art to continue His work inside me, teaching me, healing me, changing me. For in a period of minutes I found myself filled with love for a man I had disliked heartily before.

Once again it had been the Word of God which spoke to me so clearly. This phrase leaped out: *He sent forth his word and healed them*. Was this His way of telling me I would get well? Faith that I would be healed began to turn and whirl like a small wheel within my innermost being.

5

SPIRIT TO SPIRIT

SOON AFTER THE second operation to repair the bowel situation, the infection inside me went wild. My temperature soared to 105 degrees again. When the nurses began having trouble irrigating the stomach pump inside me, the doctor discovered an abscess under the first incision. Back to surgery again for minor repair, with more blood transfusions and the continuous intravenous feedings.

One of the nurses who took care of me during that period was Mary Barton. In recent years I have been in touch with Mary, who now lives in Tucson, Arizona. She vividly recalls some of the desperate moments we shared. There was the growing problem of finding veins strong enough to take the blood transfusions and intravenous feeding. They used the wrists, the bends in both arms, the ankles, and once my big toe, a most painful solution.

During my first days in the hospital I was only aware of events going on about me at a subconscious level. Gradually I began to take a more active interest in the routines. I kept asking the nurses for pieces of ice to suck. When I once asked Mary Barton if I would ever enjoy food again, she replied, "Yes. And when you do, what would you most like to eat?"

I though a moment. "A chocolate ice cream soda."

"When the time comes, I'll see that you get it myself," she replied.

She admitted to me later that she was sure this was one promise she would not have to keep.

Another problem the doctors had in battling my infection was in finding enough blood for transfusions. There was a scarcity of my type—B-negative. Radio announcements were repeatedly made for donors but the response was poor. After my second surgery there was a tense, desperate period when the hospital sought frantically for B-negative blood to give me a transfusion. When my father heard of this need, he stood at the foot of my bed to "pray in" the person with this blood type to serve as a donor for me.

The way the Lord answers prayer is fascinating. My uncle, Jesse Scott Mullins, was a brakeman for the Pennsylvania Railroad at the time, the vibrant jolly man who used to toss me about like a sack of potatoes at picnics when I was a girl. He traveled the freights on a run that went from Terre Haute to Peoria to St. Louis and back, riding the caboose, a job that made him the most glamorous man in my life. Once he took me for a short ride in the caboose, pure enchantment for this small girl. On other occasions he would bring us some fusees, the torches railroaders would light on the tracks to warn approaching trains of an obstruction or stalled train. We would light the fusees in our backyard and have picnics by this glamorous reddish-yellow glow.

At the time of my second operation, Uncle Jesse was on his way from Peoria to Terre Haute. Later he told me the full story of what happened:

As Jesse "dead-headed" into Terre Haute, he had a sudden inner feeling that he should stop at the hospital on his way home to give a pint of blood for me. My uncle was not aware of any crisis situation at Union Hospital for B-negative blood. He didn't even know what type of blood he had. All he wanted to do was help John and me keep our hospital bills down.

It was late morning and Jesse was tired and grimy from long hours on the train. It made more sense, he told himself, to go home and shower and rest first, then go to the hospital at night during visiting hours. So he climbed into his car and headed for home. Uncle Jesse had always believed that the supernatural power of God can direct our everyday lives. Therefore, when for the second time he felt an inner nudge to head for Union Hospital, he didn't just slough it off. The feeling would not go away, so despite all his logic and common-sense reasoning, he found himself going directly to the hospital from the roundhouse.

Upon arriving at the hospital, Jesse inquired about the blood donor program and asked if his gift of blood could be credited to a patient who needed transfusions. They said this could be worked out and then drew blood to get his type. Soon a nurse rushed back in a state of urgency and said that Jess had B-negative blood which at that moment was desperately needed for me. The timing was amazing. It was God alone who did it.

The infusion of Uncle Jesse's blood helped me rally. Later he came by to tease me: "I was your uncle by marriage before. Now I'm your blood uncle."

After surviving this crisis, I began straining to be a mother and wife again. "How is Brenda doing?" I asked my parents. The reassurances that my daughter was fine didn't quite satisfy me. Mother then patiently described in detail the cookies she and Brenda had made, the four new puppies that Dusty, their family dog, had delivered and how Brenda was helping Dusty keep track of her new offspring.

Several times Brenda and Gary had been put on the phone to talk to me. I heard from Gary how Brenda had hogged the one fishing pole when they went to the lake and from Brenda how she had helped Daddy and Papaw teach Gary to water-ski.

Since hospital rules forbade children under fourteen from visiting patients, the next evening they took her to the hospital lawn. "You and Mamaw sit here on the grass by those petunias," my father said, "and when I get to your Mommie's room I'll wave out the window to you. She's on the third floor. Count over four windows from the end and watch for me."

"Will Mama wave out the window, too?" Brenda wanted to know.

"Not today, but soon," Dad replied.

When he announced that Brenda was outside, I could barely nod my head. "Will someone be sure that Brenda gets to see the fireworks on the Fourth of July?" I asked.

Gently my father told me that it was now the sixth of July and that Brenda had already gotten to see the fireworks. Somehow I had lost several days.

In some ways I was more troubled about John than Brenda. My husband followed a certain ritual when he visited me. He would come into my room, kiss me lightly on the forehead or cheek, pat my arm, and then restlessly walk about or assume his sitting position on the other side of the door.

One day when he came into the room I held on to his hand. "Please stay close to me, John," I whispered. Then, summoning up all my strength, I reminded him of the miracle of Brenda.

John and I sat there reminiscing, our minds going back seven years. We had already been married four years without children. The doctor's report had been discouraging. Because of the rheumatic fever John had suffered at age nine and a later hernia condition, John's sperm count had reached an almost zero fertility rate.

We had not given in to this verdict. Once when the pastor in our church asked people to come forward for special prayer, John was the first in line. He had never told me until later that this was a request that he become a father.

While John was praying in church, I would talk to God about the situation every day in my bedroom. One morning I was reading the book of Isaiah. Suddenly these words sprang from the pages:

> For I will pour water upon him that is thirsty,
> and floods upon the dry ground:
> I will pour my spirit upon thy seed,
> and my blessing upon thine offspring.

> (Isaiah 44:3, KJV)

What a blessed promise! To think that the Lord would pour His Spirit and blessing on John and me. It was an awesome moment. I knew then that He was beginning to prepare me for motherhood.

Six weeks later I broke the news to John that I was pregnant. He wept as he told me for the first time how hard he had prayed for this to happen.

Then came a crisis during the fourth month after a long automobile trip to spend Thanksgiving dinner with John's grandparents. The next morning I began hemorrhaging and called the doctor who came and examined me. He put me to bed but warned that it was probably too late to save the baby. I did not give up. Before going to bed John and I prayed for the Lord to save our child. I rarely dream but that night I saw Jesus coming toward me, holding a tiny baby in His arms.

I started to cry, thinking that I had miscarried and that Jesus had taken the child with Him to heaven. But I was wrong: Jesus walked slowly toward me and laid the child in my arms. I awoke the next morning arms folded across my stomach, still holding the baby inside my body.

Six months later on Father's Day, June 21, 1953, Brenda was born, a healthy and normal baby in every way.

Remembering how God had spared our unborn child strengthened John. From then on he stayed inside the room and was much more relaxed. One day he came in after spending the day with Brenda. I was asleep when he arrived, but soon awoke as John began relating his experiences to my Dad.

"Brenda and I really had fun today," he said. "I took her home so she could play for a while with her old friends, with her toys and in her sand pile. Then I took her to the station. She wanted to wash some car windows, so I let her do it with customers I knew well. She had a ball.

"On the way home, I told her I would cook supper and asked her what she wanted. She told me 'Sandburgers.'" (This was Brenda's term for a hamburger sandwich.)

At this point I was so interested I opened my eyes and tried to focus on my husband. John had never fixed a meal even once in our marriage, and would have been horrified if asked to put on an apron. He would not know where to find the salt and pepper, much less how to put meat into a skillet and use the stove correctly.

But I could see that John was relaxed and enjoying his role as storyteller. "So, Brenda and I stopped at the store, grabbed a cart, and bought some groceries. When we got home, I spread out the hamburger, tomatoes, lettuce, onion, and mustard on the table. Then I got a frying pan, and opened the package of hamburger, formed a nice little 'sandburger' for Brenda and put it in the skillet.

"My first mistake. I had picked up ground pork sausage, instead of hamburger. Oh, well. Smothered with lettuce, tomatoes, onions and mustard, Brenda wouldn't know the difference.

"My second mistake. When I opened the cellophane around the lettuce I saw it was cabbage. Oh, well. Lettuce and cabbage are almost the same thing. So I fried the patty, put the sausage on the cabbage, plus all the other stuff, and served it to Brenda.

"Poor kid. She took one bite, pushed it aside and said, 'Daddy, I like gravy. Will you make me some gravy and put it on bread pieces for me? That'll be okay, Daddy.' I could see that this kid still had faith in me.

"I thought making gravy would be a breeze. . . . Just add some flour to that stuff in the skillet. Well, I must have put in too much flour. It was awful thick. Brenda took one bite and said, 'Hey, Daddy, I got it. Let's go to the Royal Chef.'

"That sounded like a great idea to me. But before we left, I didn't want to throw away all that good gravy. So I dumped it out in the cat's bowl. Pumpkin Face had been staring at us hungrily ever since we brought her over from the neighbors for the day. Well, Pumpkin Face took one lick, shivered, and walked away. The ingratitude of that cat!"

My father was laughing so hard he almost fell out of his chair. It didn't seem quite that funny to me, but it was good to see that John was getting back his sense of humor. And I was reassured over how much my family needed me.

Later that night I found myself dreaming. John was in the kitchen frying "sandburgers" and there was this awful smoke coming from the stove. I was in bed and couldn't move. . . . I tried desperately to get out of bed, but my legs seemed paralyzed. . . . I kept trying to call John to turn off the oven, but I could not open my mouth.

I woke up in a panic. My hospital room was dark; only a dim light filtered through the slightly ajar door. Desperately I reached out for the warm Presence that had comforted me during bad moments in recent days. "Lord, help me. Lord, will I ever get well? Please take away the pain."

At once the throbbing in my head eased slightly. My panic subsided. I was not alone. The Comforter had returned. Then gently, but firmly, I felt Him probing into my life again. "What did you learn today from your husband?" The question was there in my mind and I'm sure I didn't ask it of myself. My husband's pathetic effort to cook a meal showed how much he needed me.

"That's what you want, isn't it, Betty? To have your family totally dependent on you?"

Again this thought had come from the outside. It was a bit disconcerting; but not nearly as disturbing as the next thought.

"When John and Brenda are so dependent on you, Betty, they do not need Me."

By now I was wide awake. This thought deeply disturbed me. Was I blocking my husband and daughter from God?

I fought off a desire to turn away from these painful revelations about myself, but there was no condemnation in the Presence. Only loving concern. Then it seemed that the two of us were seated side by side in front of a screen on which a series of scenes from my life were flashed.

Scene: My parents, younger brothers and I are driving in our old Hudson car to church on a hot summer day. The car has no air conditioning, yet I angrily shout at my sweltering brothers that the windows must be kept shut or my hairdo will be ruined.

Scene: Our kitchen soon after my marriage to John. At 5:30 a.m. I am baking biscuits when John sleepily appears, asking why the early rising. "I want your mother to know that you have a wife who gets up early every morning to fix your breakfast."

Scene: In a local department store I spend hours trying to find matching mother-daughter outfits for Brenda and me. I explain the intensity of my search to the clerk: "It gives my daughter a sense of security to dress like her mommy."

Scene: Late at night in our bedroom. I give the room a romantic aura by lighting some candles. Next comes a spray of perfume. John watches me from the bed with mixed emotions. "Just one time I'd like you to forget the trappings, come into my arms and say that all you really want is me," he says.

Scene: John and I are talking one evening in our home. He has met a young husband and wife who have had such marital troubles that their infidelities are well known about town. "They're looking for help," says John, "and I'd like to have them for dinner and then take them to our church afterwards." I tell John that the neighbors might think it strange if we identify with people of low reputation, that it would be best for them to go to church directly and have my father minister to their needs.

All of these scenes on the surface might seem fairly typical of family life. Yet as each one flashed before me I was gently made aware of a truth about myself.

My determination to protect my hairdo in the car, at the expense of others, was not only self-centeredness, it was the beginning of a pattern to get my own way.

My early arising to bake biscuits was not to show John how much I loved him, but to impress others with what a good wife I was.

My great search to find matching mother-daughter outfits was not for Brenda's security as much as an effort to tie my daughter closer to me.

The candles and perfume act was not to make it easier for me to give myself more completely to my husband. It was a bit of fantasy on my part to make our physical relationship seem better than it was and to give me story material to impress others with the romantic quality of our marriage.

My turndown of the adulterous couple was the most devastating scene of all. Seeing my self-righteousness and pride made me want to hide my head under the pillow in shame. How this act must have grieved the Spirit of God. Tears flowed down my cheeks. "Forgive me, Lord. Forgive me."

The Presence did not have to say a word, nor did He try to soften the impact. I felt awed by the exposure of my selfish, arrogant nature. When the tears of repentance came, there was comfort and reassurance in His manner. And then once again I saw on the screen His Word for me in clear block letters: *Thou shalt have no other gods before me.*

The image faded; the Presence was gone. I raised myself from my pillow slightly to look about my hospital room. The hum of the window air-conditioner was unchanged. The bottle of liquid nourishment suspended behind my head continued to drip-drip through the tubing into my veins. The drain from my abdominal cavity continued to draw off poison into a jar underneath the bed. Everything was unchanged outside of myself. Inside I was different. I reached the call button to ask the nurse for another small piece of ice for my parched lips.

6

THE CRISIS POINT

THE DAYS WENT by; the month of July was almost over. Six weeks had passed since the first attack of appendicitis. Yet I was still fighting for my life as doctors tried different drugs to clean out the poison in my system. By now I had gone through four rounds of surgery, and my weight was down to eighty pounds. John and my parents were near exhaustion from the daily bedside rituals.

I learned later that the final crisis was brought on by pneumonia. What little resistance I had left was sharply eroded by this new invasion of germs. Nurse Mary Barton had the shift from 3:00 to 11:00 p.m. and was monitoring my vital signs carefully. Both Dad and Mother were in the room the afternoon of the emergency.

It happened around 4:30 p.m. Mary had come in to check the IV equipment because several times when the needle had been inserted, a collapsed vein had rejected the fluids. Little bubbles had formed in several places on my skin where this had happened.

Suddenly she grabbed my hand and took my pulse. There was none. Startled, she looked at the pupils of my eyes. Then she called for emergency equipment. All my parents could do was watch helplessly and pray.

There followed a tense desperate drama as both the doctor on duty and several nurses used emergency measures to get my heart, pulse and blood pressure functioning again. By the time my vital signs were back to normal Dr. Bherne and John had arrived. The strain was too much for Mother. She fainted and a nurse ministered to her. The doctor then pulled my father aside and told him that he felt it would be only a matter of hours before I slipped away. He said quite frankly that death might be the best solution. He suspected that I might have such severe brain damage, plus the extensive assault on other internal organs by gangrene, that I could never live a normal life.

Depressed and exhausted, Dad decided to drive my mother home, get some sleep and return early the next morning. John, who was now spending his nights at my parents' home with Brenda, decided he would close his Sunoco station early and join Mother and Dad and the children for a late supper.

Here again, I learned about the events which followed from my parents, especially Dad. And it was strange how certain experiences in Dad's early life were to affect the present crisis.

During the thirty-one-mile drive back to their home in Clay City, Mother did most of the talking. "I just can't believe God wants to take a vital twenty-seven-year-old woman from her husband and daughter. She's needed here, Glenn. Why, Betty has only begun to live."

"God doesn't take a young wife away from her husband and child in a cold-blooded manner, Fern," my father answered. "Often we don't understand why things happen the way they do until later, but we know that we must trust Him to do what's best in the long run for His children."

"But God can heal Betty?"

"Yes. He certainly can."

"Then let's keep praying that He will."

In a few minutes, Mother's depression returned. "Where will we bury Betty? Do you think John will let us bury her in our family plot—or will he want a plot of his own?"

Once again my father tried to comfort Mother; both were silent during the rest of the drive home.

As Dad walked into his study, his first thought was to read something from Scripture. Then he noticed on his desk five cards lined up in a row—five Father's Day remembrances received many weeks before from each of his children, four sons and one daughter. Once again he read the words I had written to him:

Dear Daddy,

Happy Papa's Day to thee! . . . from me! You have been more than a Dad. You've been a priest and teacher too. I didn't realize until I became a parent myself, how much like Jesus you are. You are the son of a carpenter, as He was, learning to work with your hands with wood and shavings . . . even building churches both structurally and spiritually.

There are men who sire children, but are not fathers. There are mothers who are merely incubators. You and Mother have nurtured me, introduced me to God. You were my first church, and this child's first university.

> Your ugliest daughter,
> (the only one too)
> Betsy

Tears streaming down his face, Dad told me later how he sat there for a long time, praying for the faith to believe that his only daughter could get well. Then he remembered another time years before when he had no faith at all. Glenn Perkins was twenty-two, newly married, and barely making a living back in 1930 as a mechanic in a glass factory. His young wife, Fern, was desperately sick with uremic poisoning. Her fingernails had turned purple. The doctor had packed her in ice to bring down her temperature and felt an operation might give her a fifty-fifty chance to live.

A group of Fern's church friends and the pastor came to pray. They were so noisy about it that Glenn, a nonbeliever, took off for the woods. Hours later he returned to find his wife standing in the middle of the room singing hymns and praising God. She had been healed.

After this example of a miracle-working God, Glenn Perkins began studying the Bible and attending services. One night he was reading the second chapter of Acts.

"Suddenly the black Bible began to glow in my hands," he told us later. "It seemed to be on fire. Then the house began to shake. It was the Upper Room all over again. I shouted at Fern: 'Pray for me, honey. Something's wrong.' I didn't know what to do. I didn't think I could stand it."

At the next church service my father went forward and accepted Jesus Christ as Savior and Lord. When this happened, I was six months old.

Dad then began attending Bible school in his spare time, while making a living as a carpenter. In the fall of 1932 my father was impressed by a visiting preacher named Kenneth Wilkerson, who was starting a new church in nearby Attica, Indiana. Wilkerson's congregation was meeting above a grocery store. Dad was hired as a carpenter by Pastor Wilkinson to help build a new church, using volunteers from the congregation.

It was a severe winter, volunteers were scarce and Kenneth Wilkerson and my father did most of the construction themselves. It was so cold and money was so scarce that Dad often had to round up sacks of dried corncobs from a feed mill to burn in the potbellied stove to keep them warm while they worked. When the church was finished, my father stayed on to assist Kenneth Wilkerson, teaching, leading the singing, and counseling young people.

One of Kenneth Wilkerson's sons was a boy named David. He was a mixed-up youth, bored with the church and skeptical of the spiritual convictions of his parents. Then the Holy Spirit touched David Wilkerson and revolutionized his life. Later, when David was led by God to come to New York City to minister to disturbed teenagers, this marked the beginning of Teen Challenge and formed the basis for *The Cross and the Switchblade*, David Wilkerson's internationally bestselling book.

Although he could barely provide for his family during those depression years of the thirties, my father could not deny the call of God on his life. As he sat at his desk praying for me that bleak summer night in 1959, feeling strong assaults on his faith, Dad remembered another occasion when the Lord used him in a dramatic way.

It happened in the middle of a snowy night in the early thirties. Dad suddenly awoke. One unsuccessful effort to go back to sleep made him realize that the Lord had awakened him and wanted him to do something. Mother was sleeping serenely beside him, and everything in the house seemed to be in order.

Then he was given a message in the form of a clear, strong inner directive. He was told to go down to the business district of west Terre Haute. Someone was there in desperate need. This was a time when Indiana was hard-hit by the depression.

At first, Dad was not sure that he had heard correctly. Would he not feel foolish dressing and going to town in the middle of the night? What if he found nothing but snowy, deserted streets?

Kneeling down by the bed, he asked for verification of what he thought he had heard. Immediately, he felt God's presence and lines from a hymn were dropped into his mind:

> Rescue the perishing,
> Care for the dying . . .

By then Mother was awake. He explained what had happened, got dressed, bundled up, and started for town.

As he strode along briskly, trying to keep warm, he wondered what he would do if there were several people on the streets. How would he know the person he was being sent to help? He concluded that if God would send him on an errand like this, He could surely be trusted to handle such details.

When Dad got to the main street there was but one person in sight, a man leaning against a lamppost, his head down. With a quick prayer, asking the Lord to protect and guide him, Dad approached the stranger. "Is there any way I can help you?"

The man must have seen kindness and compassion in Dad's face for the story came pouring out. "My wife and I have quarreled because I can't make a living for my family. I've tried and tried, but I can't find a job. I'm useless, worthless. I've been trying to decide whether to lie down in front of the early morning fright or kill myself with this gun in my pocket. But I *am* going to end it all."

He paused for breath, his eyes searching Dad's face. "Sir, I'd like to ask you, what would you do if you were me?"

Promptly came the answer. "Sir, if it were me, I would turn my life over to Almighty God who loves me and who has promised to supply all my needs."

The two men talked earnestly for a while, then knelt down on the snowy sidewalk while the desperate man handed his life over to Jesus. He then went home to his family and began a new life.

Dad told us later, "I've scarcely ever felt such joy as at that moment. It seemed that all of Heaven was shouting hosannas. I know something of Jesus' great joy when in our extremity, any of us allows Him to be our Savior and gives Him the chance to save us from our problems."

My father went into the fulltime ministry soon after that experience and became a loving, patient, sensitive pastor beloved by his flock.

When John arrived, Mother and Dad rounded up Gary and Brenda and at eight o'clock the five had a subdued meal together. The children had questions which no one wanted to answer. What was there to say? Everyone was taut with fatigue and discouragement. John's silence and the haunted look on his face especially troubled Dad, he told me later.

Then Dad asked everyone to hold hands around the table as he prayed: "Lord Jesus, we love You and praise You for the good things of life You have given us. We thank You for Betty, for trusting us with her these years. We relinquish her to You now, knowing how much You love her too. Be with her now, Lord, as she struggles for life. Mend her body, soothe her mind, heal her spirit. Forgive us for our lack of faith and our weaknesses, Lord. We want only to serve You. Amen."

At 3:30 a.m. Dad suddenly awoke. A look at his watch told him it was too early to get up. But when he tried to close his

eyes, he felt the same inner prodding he had years before on that snowy night in the middle of the depression.

The Lord was asking him to get up and go now to the hospital. Betty needed him!

My father arose, shaved, dressed and had some toast and a cup of coffee. He then woke John. When he slipped out of the house it was about 4:15 a.m. Dad took Highway 41 from Clay City direct to southern Terre Haute and Union Hospital. The drive took him about forty-five minutes. John left a few minutes later for his station.

Shortly after 5:00 a.m. the telephone awakened my mother. She answered in sudden panic. The woman introduced herself as the night nurse on the third floor of Union Hospital.

"Mrs. Perkins, I'm sorry to call you at this hour, but I have bad news. Your daughter, Betty, passed away a few minutes ago. We can't reach her husband. Will you try and locate him and ask him to come to the hospital as soon as possible to make the necessary arrangements? If Mr. Upchurch can't be reached, will you ask your husband to come to the hospital as soon as possible?"

Mother pulled herself together as best she could. "My husband is on his way to the hospital right now. Please intercept him before he goes to Betty's room. Seeing his daughter's body will be a great shock for him."

The nurse promised she would be on the lookout for Dad and hung up. Mother lay down on her pillow and sobbed.

In his own words, here is Dad's account of what happened when he arrived at the hospital:

"It was still dark when I parked my car near the back of the hospital. The time: about 5:00 a.m. There were faint streaks of light in the sky as I walked toward the nurses' entrance because it was a much more direct route to Betty's room. I climbed the two flights of stairs and headed for Betty's room, number 336. Down the hall, I saw the black nurses' aide leave Betty's room and close the door. This was unusual; always before the door had been open.

"I knocked softly on Betty's door. There was no answer. I opened the door and walked inside.

"The room seemed very dark and still. And empty. As my eyes adjusted to the gloom, I first noticed the absence of the life-supporting equipment. Startled, my eyes swung to the bed.

"A sheet had been pulled up over Betty's head!

"Slowly the facts worked to a conclusion in my mind: Betty was dead. I stood there for several minutes in frozen silence as feelings of grief flooded my emotions. Then all that I felt focused on one word which I spoke several times fervently.

"'Jesus . . . Jesus . . . Jesus.'

"It was a plea, a moan and a prayer. It was also the only word that ever made sense to me in times of great bewilderment, or pain or sorrow. I don't know how long I stood there beside the bed. I only remember that the room lightened as the sun began to slip through the curtains.

"Then my eyes were caught by something. Did I see a slight movement in the sheet covering Betty?"

7

THE CITY OF TOMORROW

MY MEMORY OF the late-afternoon crisis and the rest of that day is blurred. Dimly I recall a crowded room, slipping into a coma, then coming out of it. I was vaguely aware that my parents left my hospital room first, John sometime later, that Nurse Barton watched me closely before she went off duty, that a young nurse's aide was in and out of my room during the night.

It must have been sometime around 5:00 a.m. when my body functions apparently stopped, much as they had earlier in the day. Only this time there was no one at my bedside to call for the emergency equipment.

The transition was serene and peaceful. I was walking up a beautiful green hill. It was steep, but my leg motion was effortless and a deep ecstasy flooded my body. Despite three incisions in my body from the operations, I stood erect without pain, enjoying my tallness, free from inhibitions about it. I looked down. I seemed to be barefoot, but the complete outer shape of my body was a blur and colorless. Yet I was walking on grass, the most vivid shade of green I had ever seen. Each blade was perhaps one inch long, the texture like fine velvet; every blade was vibrant and moving. As the bottoms of my feet touched the grass, something alive in the grass was transmitted up through my whole body with each step I took.

"Can this be death?" I wondered. If so, I certainly had nothing to fear. There was no darkness, no uncertainty, only a change in location and a total sense of well-being.

All around me was a magnificent deep blue sky, unobscured by clouds. Looking about, I realized that there was no road or path. Yet I seemed to know where to go.

Then I realized I was not walking alone. To the left, and a little behind me, strode a tall, masculine-looking figure in a robe. I wondered if he were an angel and tried to see if he had wings. But he was facing me and I could not see his back. I sensed, however, that he could go anywhere he wanted and very quickly.

We did not speak to each other. Somehow it didn't seem necessary, for we were both going in the same direction. Then I became aware that he was not a stranger. He knew me and I felt a strange kinship with him. Where had we met? Had we always known each other? It seemed we had. Where were we now going?

As we walked together I saw no sun—but light was everywhere. Off to the left there were multicolored flowers blooming. Also trees, shrubs. On the right was a low stone wall.

Once years before I had climbed to the top of Logan's Pass in Glacier National Park, breathing the pure, clean, unused air amidst the snowcapped peaks. There were small flowers blooming even in the snow. My legs had been sore and tired from that climb.

This climb was different. My legs were not tired and I wasn't aware of any temperature. There was no snow, though I seemed to be in a high altitude. There seemed to be no seasons but it felt like early spring. My emotion was a combination of feelings: youth, serenity, fulfillment, health, awareness, tranquility. I felt I had everything I ever wanted to have. I was everything I had ever intended to be. I was arriving at where I had always dreamed of being.

The wall to my right was higher now and made of many-colored, multi-tiered stones. A light from the other side of the wall shone through a long row of amber-colored gems several feet above my head. "Topaz," I thought to myself. "The November birthstone." I remembered this from working in Edwards Jewelry store in New Castle, Indiana, before my marriage to John. November 6th is my birthday.[1]

Just as we crested the top of the hill, I heard my father's voice calling, "Jesus, Jesus, Jesus." His voice was a long distance away. I thought about turning back to find him. I did not because I knew my destination was ahead. We walked along in silence save for the whisper of a gentle breeze ruffling the white, sheer garments of the angel.

We came upon a magnificent, silver structure. It was like a palace except there were no towers. As we walked toward it, I heard voices. They were melodious, harmonious, blending in chorus and I heard the word, "Jesus." There were more than four parts to their harmony. I not only heard the singing and felt the singing but I joined the singing. I have always had a girl's body, but a low boy's voice. Suddenly I realized I was

---

1. Editor's note: Betty was later to discover that the 21st chapter of Revelation, verses 19–20, described the heavenly city whose walls were to be adorned with precious stones. The first foundation was jasper; the second sapphire . . . the ninth, topaz. If each foundation was about a foot high, this would place topaz about three feet higher than Betty's head.

singing the way I had always wanted to . . . in high, clear, and sweet tones.

After a while the music softened, then the unseen voices picked up a new chorus. The voices not only burst forth in more than four parts, but they were in different languages. I was awed by the richness and perfect blending of the words—and I could understand them! I do not know why this was possible except that I was part of a universal experience.

While the angel and I walked together I sensed we could go wherever we willed ourselves to go and be there instantly. Communication between us was through the projection of thoughts. The words sung in all the different languages were understandable, but I don't know how or why. We all seemed to be on some universal wave length.

I thought at the time, "I will never forget the melody and these words." But later I could only recall two: "Jesus" and "redeemed."

The angel stepped forward and put the palm of his hand upon a gate which I had not noticed before. About twelve feet high, the gate was a solid sheet of pearl, with no handles and some lovely scroll work at the top of its Gothic structure. The pearl was translucent so that I could almost, but not quite, see inside. The atmosphere inside was somehow filtered through. My feeling was of ecstatic joy and anticipation at the thought of going inside.

When the angel stepped forward, pressing his palm on the gate, an opening appeared in the center of the pearl panel and slowly widened and deepened as though the translucent material was dissolving. Inside I saw what appeared to be a street of golden color with an overlay of glass or water. The yellow light that appeared was dazzling. There is no way to describe it. I saw no figure, yet I was conscious of a

Person. Suddenly I knew that the light was Jesus, the Person was Jesus.

I did not have to move. The light was all about me. There seemed to be some heat in it as if I were standing in sunlight; my body began to glow. Every part of me was absorbing the light. I felt bathed by the rays of a powerful, penetrating, loving energy.

The angel looked at me and communicated the thought: "Would you like to go in and join them?"

I longed with all my being to go inside, yet I hesitated. Did I have a choice? Then I remembered my father's voice. Perhaps I should go and find him.

"I would like to stay and sing a little longer, then go back down the hill!" I finally answered. I started to say something more. But it was too late.

The gates slowly melted into one sheet of pearl again and we began walking back down the same beautiful hill. This time the jeweled wall was on my left and the angel walked on my right.

Then I saw the sun coming up over the wall. This surprised me since it was already very light and there seemed to be no passing of time. It was a lovely sunrise. The topaz and other stones glowed brilliantly. I remember noticing that the wall now made a deep shadow on my side.

Walking down the hill I looked into Terre Haute as the worlds of spirit and time and space began to fuse back together. Ahead of me were many church steeples glistening in the morning sun. I was suddenly aware of God's love for all His churches. It was a sudden bit of knowledge, as if I were being told this on the inside by the Holy Spirit. At that moment I loved all His churches too; and as my prejudices dissolved, I loved all His people.

Then I saw the tops of trees, then the hospital. My eyes seemed to bore through the walls of the hospital like laser beams, down the hall of the third floor to Room 336. I saw a figure on the bed with a sheet pulled over it.

After my descent I slowed down and stopped. The sun's rays were in my eyes. There were dust particles in the light which suddenly changed to wavy letters about two inches high flashing before me like a ticker-tape message. The letters seemed composed of translucent ivory, only fluid—moving through the rays of sun.

I was back in my hospital bed now and the letters stretched all the way from the window, past my bed and on into the room. They read: *I am the resurrection and the life; he that believeth in me, though he were dead, yet shall he live.*

The words were so alive that they pulsated. I knew that I had to touch those living words. I reached up and out and pushed the sheet off my face. At that instant the Word of God literally became life to me. The warmth in the moving letters flowed into my fingers and up my arm. I sat up in bed!

No man can claim credit for my healing. *The Lord had sent forth His WORD and healed me* (Ps. 107:20). Days before, the man Art had read this Scripture at the foot of my bed.

Promise became reality . . . hope became fact.

My father was staring at me in a state of shock. I noticed him only for a moment. I was still seeking out the unearthly light in the room, determined to find its source. My eyes went to the window. Outside was a glorious sight—the green grass on the lawn of the hospital. I had been too sick to see it before, too busy for years to notice how beautiful green grass can be.

Then I saw another beautiful sight outside. A black man. He was carrying on his shoulder a case of soft drinks into the building. I had never before cared for black people. Yet I now felt a great love for that man. God was continuing His healing work in me.

At last I looked at my father standing by my bed. He was still stunned, too startled to cry out, or hug me, or shed tears of joy. Rather he was rooted to the spot, struck dumb with awe before the majesty of the working of God.

8

MY CHANGED WORLD

I TRIED TO TELL Dad about the experience I had just been through on the other side, but I don't think he really heard me. He just kept smiling at me and squeezing my hand, tears sliding down his cheeks. His eyes seemed to devour me.

When the young nurse's aide popped into the room and saw me sitting up in bed, she screamed, "Ma'am, you're a ghost!" Her black face was ashen. I reached for her hand, surprised by the warm feeling inside that made me want to hug her and reassure her. "Tell the floor nurse, I'm not only alive, but I feel wonderful."

The young aide scurried away and soon the chief nurse, with a shocked expression on her face, was wheeling back into the room the life support equipment that had been removed. Jubilant calls were made to John, who had just arrived at the station, and Mother.

The nurses wanted to put the tubes back in me but I shook my head. "I'm sure I don't need them any more. I'm hungry. Please tell Dr. Bherne that I want some real food."

Then I picked up the telephone and dialed my elderly paternal grandmother, Mom Perky. She was in her eighties, a gentle, old-fashioned servant of the Lord. "Hello, Mom Perky, this is Betty! Do you believe in miracles? I'm sitting up here in bed feeling great." God love her, she was so confused. She had been ill for a long time and Mother had called just a short time before to tell her I had died. She now thought we were both in heaven and talking there on the phone.

Minutes later John arrived in my room, so moved he didn't quite know what to do. He stood next to Dad, staring at me, trying to understand the journey I had taken. Every now and then he would reach over and pat me on the shoulder, or on my knee or the arm, or my side to see if I was real.

There sure wasn't much left of me—just an emaciated yellowish-green face and a skinny disintegrated eighty-pound skeleton of a body. But how alive I felt!

Dr. Bherne was the next to arrive. I'll probably never know what conversation took place between him and the floor nurse before he walked into my room. He gave me a long, careful look, paying little attention to my excited chatter. Then he began a careful examination. I noticed a tremor in his hand when he applied the stethoscope. Finally, he flashed me a cautious smile.

"You are indeed much better," he said.

"The Lord has healed me," I replied. "I died about an hour ago. I met Him over there and He let me return. It was in incredibly beautiful experience."

The doctor looked uncomfortable. "Some things happen which we can't explain. Whatever it was—you seem to be much improved."

"How do you explain my sudden recovery?"

He smiled, "I believe in things I can personally explain."

Several of my relatives arrived and the doctor started to leave. "Before you go, Dr. Bherne, I want you to know that I'm very hungry. When do I eat real food?"

It was the first time I had wanted solid food since the night of the bad pain down in Florida.

The doctor shook his head. "You must go very slow on that. Perhaps some 7-Up on ice to start."

The festive air continued in my room all morning as a stream of relatives arrived. It was a victory party. Two more doctors appeared to examine and question me. But the 7-Up on ice never appeared.

Around noon the young nurse's aide brought me a tray. On it were two pork chops, applesauce, cottage cheese, a square of lemon cake with warm sauce and a pot of tea. Hungrily I ate every morsel, thinking it the most delicious food I ever tasted.

Shortly thereafter a flustered nurse came in to examine my tray, pursued by an irate patient named Mrs. Underwood who had been served nothing but a few ounces of 7-Up for lunch. Upchurch and Underwood—it was easy to see how the mix-up occurred. Sure enough, behind the teapot on my tray was a card with Underwood on it.

Minutes later the nurse returned with a mobile unit. "I'm sorry. I'm going to have to pump out your stomach."

Every fiber of my body protested that this was not necessary. "Please . . . please," I insisted. "The food was so good. It went down so smoothly and I feel just fine."

The nurse continued unrolling the tubing. "Orders are orders," she replied.

"I'm sorry," I said more firmly. "But I have lost so much weight that this nourishment is desperately needed." She wavered. "I promise to ring you the moment I think I'm in trouble," I continued.

Reluctantly, the nurse retreated with her unit. "Lord," I prayed, "please help digest this food."

The process of eating, digestion and elimination is so routine with most of us that we never appreciate what a miraculously smooth operation it is until something goes wrong. The next few hours was a time of great suspense. I hadn't eaten real food in weeks. Would the pork and applesauce and cottage cheese pass through the digestive tract? If there was a problem, my stomach would quickly flash the warning signal.

Several hours went by as relatives continued to come and go. The body gave its sign and I pushed the call button. When the nurse appeared apprehensively, I flashed her my brightest smile. "Would you help me to the bathroom, please?"

Wobbly as I was, it was like a triumphant procession. And how can I describe my jubilation to find that all my plumbing worked?

The next morning Dr. Bherne closed the door to my room, examined me carefully and then sat down in a chair by the bed. Seeing that he had also adjusted a second chair near his, I pointed to it. "Anyone else coming to this pity party? Or is it a welcome back party?"

He laughed for the first time. "That chair there is for gangrene to set in!" he replied humorously.

I laughed too. How good it sounded!

I liked Dr. Bherne. He had been very negative about my chances; he was a somber man, but a fine doctor, a skilled surgeon. I felt a sudden burst of gratitude for the hours of care he had given me.

Now I really saw him for the first time; a short man with rimless eyeglasses, furrowed brow, graying thinning hair closely cropped. His eyes were friendly, but somewhat disapproving. I sensed he was about to give a sober serious talk about what the illness had done to me.

"I think we can release you from the hospital in a few days," he began. "This is good news, of course. We are delighted by your comeback. But you have been a desperately sick woman for a long time. It will be many months before we know the extent of the damage to your system." Then he went on to tick off the areas which were of concern to him. It seemed that the infection had collided with nearly every organ in my body.

"We did not remove your reproductive organs," he continued, "but I could tell that they were severely damaged by the gangrenous infection. There is such a thin membrane between the appendix and the ovaries that peritonitis is always a severe threat to a woman's fertility. In your case, there is hardly one chance in a hundred that you could conceive, one in a thousand that the baby would be normal. In fact, the odds are probably even worse than that.

"I strongly urge you and your husband to use contraceptives from now on. Considering the massive infection which bombarded your ovaries, I also suggest that you consider having them removed sometime soon. A deformed child is quite a price to pay for carelessness, although I do not believe there is much chance you could conceive under any circumstances."

When he had finished his lecture, the doctor gave me that approving smile he reserved for cooperative patients and left to make his rounds.

It was several days before Nurse Mary Barton returned to duty. She came into the room, stood at the foot of my bed and stared at me, speechless and wide-eyed while I described the healing I had received.

"I just can't believe it," she said. "You were dying when I last saw you." She picked up my chart and stared at it in disbelief. "And you're now back on solid food, too."

All I could do was grin at the bewilderment on her kind face.

Later that afternoon, on her coffee break, Mary crossed the street, entered the fountain of the Walgreen Drug Store and purchased a large chocolate ice cream soda. With a giant-sized smile on her face, Mary Barton then appeared in my room and presented it to me with a great flourish, making good on her promise. "This is one bet I never thought I'd have to pay off," she said.

What a treat it was! I don't know who enjoyed it the most: Mary, the grinning gift-bearer, or Betty, the eager recipient.

Several days later John brought me home. It took two trips to carry the accumulation of flowers, plants, gifts, and personal items. I was still so frail and weak that I could only take a few steps at a time. But what a thrill for John and me to be back in our own home, to lie again together in our bed, to sit across the breakfast table, to hold hands on the living room couch as we watched television, to see Brenda dashing about the house with her dolls and toys, telling friends excitedly, "Mommy's home! Mommy's home!"

What a difference I felt now about my home. Gone was the restlessness, the desire to escape to Florida. Instead, there was a steady continuous feeling of praise. In the hospital the Lord had first helped me see myself and my sinful nature and then through His Word He had shown me what correction was needed. How wonderful to have this personal relationship with Him. How incredible to encounter Jesus personally in His world and to stand in His light and feel the marvelous flow of His health pass through my body!

I began each day with Him, absorbing more of His Word, seeking His Presence with a joyful sound on my lips. One morning as I was to start a recuperative program, there came a clear message on the mirror of my mind: *You shall be like a tree planted by the water.*

Quickly I reached for my Bible and turned to the First Psalm, which is a tribute to the righteous man. There it was—third verse:

> And he shall be like a tree planted by the rivers of
>   water,
> that bringeth forth his fruit in his season;
> his leaf also shall not wither;
> and whatsoever he doeth shall prosper.
>
>   (KJV)

The more I meditated on this, the more I felt that the Lord would have me key on the word "water," that He was advising me to drink six to eight glasses a day to continue the flushing out of impurities in my system. My skin, my tissue, all my organs were crying for moisture. It is a procedure I have followed to this day, resulting in a long period of good health, no colds, clear skin. Thank You, Lord! (A man who heard me tell about this in a speech wrote me recently that he had been unable to wear contact lenses until he began drinking six to eight glasses of water per day. Results: more moisture in his eyes and the irritation gone.)

During the months that followed, I slowly built up my body, regained lost weight and watched carefully for problems that Dr. Bherne indicated I might have. There were no aftereffects to the pain-killing drugs. My body functions were normal. My eyesight seemed unimpaired.

Some years later I went to the Bureau of Motor Vehicles to renew my drivers' license. I read the charts quickly and easily. The testing officer then asked me to remove my contact lenses and read the fine print on the lower line again. He could not understand the jubilation of my reply when I said, "I'll reread the lower line, but I don't wear contact lenses."

Before my illness I had a fear of high places. Looking down from a tall building made me weak, paralyzed, yet there had been no feelings of fear when I descended from God's City. Nor have I felt any apprehension of high places ever since.

John and I talked and prayed about the possibility of a malformed pregnancy resulting unless we used contraceptives. My inner guidance was that when the Lord heals, He does it completely. John was inclined to follow the doctor's advice—at least for a while. I decided to obey my husband.

The healing was not limited to my body. In addition to dealing with my restless spirit, the Lord cleansed me of lifelong prejudices toward minority groups and a distaste for certain personality types. One of the first persons I sought out was Art Lindsey to thank him personally for the therapy of his visit to me in the hospital. Next was to be Mother Upchurch.

My recuperation period was marred only by John's setback. He came home early from work one day complaining of severe fatigue and went to bed. It was so unlike John I wanted to call the doctor. John said no; he just needed a day or so of rest. Unfortunately this was the time Mother Upchurch chose to visit us.

I had been looking forward to her visit, believing my resentment was gone, determined to have a good relationship with my mother-in-law. When the bell rang late the next morning, I opened the door and embraced her warmly. She was cautiously friendly; her brown eyes studied me for a moment, then swept over the room. She missed nothing; new toys for Brenda, a scatter rug from my parents' home, my new pair of blue shoes.

The moment she entered the living room all her attention was focused on John, who was sitting in a chair in his bathrobe working on the plans for our new house. Her eyes probed every detail of his appearance. Then she launched forth, "John, I'm really worried about you. You look so pale. What's wrong? Why are you home in the middle of the day?"

As always John ignored her solicitations about his health. "I want you to see the plans for our new house," he said.

Mother looked them over, then pursed her lips. "I don't see how you can afford it." Then staring at me, "You two will forever be living beyond your means."

The visit was a disaster. Through it I learned that the healing of my emotions had obviously not gone as deep as I thought.

9

THE SETBACK

MOTHER UPCHURCH'S VISIT was a sharp reverse for me. I thought I was free of my resentment toward her. Now it was back. What bothered me most was that I sensed she was probably right about the new house and John's health, just as she had been right about my spending too much money on things, about holding me responsible for our being in debt so much of the time, and about my being evasive toward her.

But the situation was different now. I cared less about things, more about being a good wife and mother. It was John who was taking the initiative about the new house. I had tried to get John to a doctor but he refused to go. Thus I felt that her accusations toward me were unfair.

While brooding about the situation one morning, it occurred to me that there were several Scriptures that John's mother needed to read. That was the answer. The Word would convict her of her critical nature. Perhaps I should put them in a letter. I reached for a sheet of stationery, then paused.

No, the direct approach was better with my mother-in-law. She always said she liked to "call a spade a spade."

I marked the passages and placed the Bible by the telephone. A casual call making reference to the Scriptures would be the way to handle it. The first verse was in Proverbs. With my right hand ready to dial the number, my left turned the pages of the Bible to the chapter.

My eyes fell on the verse. Wait a minute! That wasn't it. Where did that verse come from? I had read through the Bible from beginning to end twice and never recalled that particular verse:

Set a watch, O Lord, before my mouth; keep the door of my lips (Ps. 141:3, KJV).

It was obvious, I had to laugh. "Lord, You're doing it to me again." I had intended to point the Word against my mother-in-law; instead the Lord turned it around so that it was pointing at me. What a sense of humor He has!

Then I realized that a telephone call wasn't the answer at all; what I really had to do was ask my mother-in-law to forgive me for years of unfriendly words, thoughts and actions against her.

We had been saving for ten years to build our dream house, the plans having been drawn up before my sickness. While John was now eager to go ahead, something inside me was resisting. I should have listened to this Inner Voice but did not and we commissioned the builder to go ahead.

Our new eight-room ranch-style house was built primarily with gray Bedford stone—long, heavy, expensive slabs from an Indiana quarry. The design centered around a lavender wrought-iron grape-leaf pattern; we worked it into the trim, shutters, window boxes, porch furniture and on all columns and porch posts. The wallpaper included lavender in the wisteria and lilacs in bloom. Our wall-to-wall carpet was a deep purple; the furniture mostly white. The foundation planting included lilac bushes and wisteria trees.

John regained his vitality following his brief illness, but I noticed his work days were shorter now. He closely supervised the building of our dream house, but did less of the actual work than was in his original plan. When finished, it was beautiful. Yet as we moved in I had no inner joy or elation, and this gave me an uneasy feeling.

One evening the following summer Brenda, now eight, and I were in our new home watching television. The TV picture kept blurring because of thunderstorms in the area. It had been a sultry humid summer day. At sunset the sky was a peculiar yellow-green. I remember wishing that John would close up his business and come home early.

Suddenly at 9:20 p.m. the television picture and sound went haywire as the storm broke overhead. When I turned the set off, a warning system went off inside me and I heard a voice: *You and Brenda get out of this room.*

I started to reason with this warning. "I've never been afraid of storms or the dark or death."

But the voice was insistent. The issue was obedience or not. I grabbed Brenda's hand and we sped from the family room into the bedroom. A moment later there was a sound like a hundred freight cars rumbling and shaking overhead. Looking up, I saw the entire roof separate and blow away from the house. The suction pasted us fast against the wall, bruising my hip. Then I flung Brenda down to the floor and threw my body across her.

The family room we had just left was gone, disintegrated. If I had not obeyed, we both would have been killed.

Brenda and I put our heads under the cherry canopy bed as eight-foot pieces of Bedford stone hurtled about us. The redwood beams broke off and piled up at crazy angles. Then came walls of water in torrents, drenching us, flooding the room so that we had to twist our necks at crazy angles to breathe. A bolt of lightning struck through the debris of our house burning a six-foot circle on the carpet near us.

Brenda was praying out loud. "Oh, Jesus, keep Mommie and me safe. Don't let Smokey (our dog) get hurt. Or Pumpkin Face (our cat). And please, Jesus, don't let my goldfish blow away."

Minutes later, when the wind and the rain stopped, the house was a total ruin. In the garage our new Cadillac car was crushed. The tornado, not even registered at the nearby airport, had destroyed or damaged thirty-six houses in our area.

But Smokey soon wiggled out unhurt from some debris. Pumpkin Face was safe under the crushed car. And to my utter astonishment the glass aquarium was still intact, filled with flecks of debris, to be sure, but all the fish were alive.

When this freakish, capricious tornado struck, I was clad in a sheer white shorty nightgown. As I was helped from the wreckage, a neighbor ran to get me her husband's terrycloth robe, which became my chief garment for the next two days. All Brenda had on was a pair of white panties, size four. In twenty seconds, the tornado had demolished possessions that had taken us ten years to accumulate.

When John arrived with the sightseers, repair crews, newspaper reporters and television cameras, we viewed the scene with awe. Plastered against one intact wall was a box of Jello sucked from the kitchen cabinet. The Bible was unruffled on the top of the coffee table, one of the few pieces of furniture that remained. The next morning a friend called to say he found our family portraits two and a half miles away in a field. After retrieving them, we returned to our cluttered yard where a reporter from *The Grit* pointed with a smile to an object at the side of our shattered home. There lying in plain view, cover and title up, was a copy of *Gone with the Wind*.

A few individuals pilfered some of our personal belongings, but most people offered help. Our church had a linen shower for us; neighbors loaned us clothing; the insurance company replaced nearly everything, including Brenda's toys; and we were able to rebuild our home within six months.

For days I went around praising Jesus. *The Lord gave, and the Lord has taken away; blessed be the name of the Lord* (Job 1:21). He really is a Savior, I thought to myself. What surprised me more than anything else was my calm at the destruction of prized personal possessions. Things did not matter to me so much since my experience in the hospital. The following verse from a hymn truly described my feelings:

> A tent or a cottage, why should I care?
> They're building a palace for me over there;
> Though exiled from home, yet, still I may sing;
> All glory to God, I'm a child of the King![2]

Some months after we had rebuilt our home, John began negotiations to buy a group of gasoline stations throughout the country. I remember the sinking feeling in my stomach when he admitted for the first time that the long hours of physical work were too much for him. Operating a chain of stations, he felt, would be less demanding.

When in 1963 John suggested that the time had come to move to Florida, I quickly agreed but for different reasons

2. Harriet E. Buell, "A Child of the King."

than I had back in 1959. Florida just might be the place for more relaxed living. So we moved to Clearwater Beach on the west coast of Florida, not too many miles from the Gulf Vista Retreat Center, the scene of my "tummy ache."

John did slow down in Florida, but not through choice. His energy level suddenly dropped again. This time he did go to the hospital for tests. The results were sobering. X-rays of John's heart showed that the aorta valve was shrinking and the heart enlarging. Doctors suggested a valve replacement operation to correct the situation. They warned him it was something he should not postpone. Reluctantly he gave up his idea of setting up a chain of gas stations.

In March of 1963 John and I both went to Gainesville, Florida, so that he could have additional tests at the J. Hillis Miller Heart Center there. We decided to make this a special "get away time" for just the two of us.

We checked into Arrowhead Lodge, which overlooked the campus of the University of Florida Medical School. Our room was on the second floor. I recall thinking that sixteen dollars a day was pretty steep, but that we were not to concern ourselves with economy. As serious as the occasion was, we were to be "joyful unto the Lord."

To this day I remember the room with its blue motif, the seascapes on the wall, the rustic brown balcony outside with its round table and old-fashioned parlor-type ice-cream chairs. We spent much of our time on this balcony, watching the student activity on the campus, talking.

The first day I could tell that my husband had a heavy load of fear on his heart, but he tried not to show it. We began discussing the medical details involved with the valve replacement operation. Heart surgery was always risky, but the doctors had assured John that the percentages were in his favor.

While we were drinking cokes together, John thought back to age nine when he had rheumatic fever. He barely remembered it. It wasn't until five years later that a doctor told him he might have a heart problem some day, but not to worry. When John heard his mother praying one night for his heart to be healed, John began to worry. Then a close friend was killed in a car wreck.

John's eyes had a far-off look. "One day he was there full of life, then my happy joyous friend was gone. I saw death then as a cheater—a robber of life. He was after me, too. Here was my very real enemy. How I hated him. Then you were near death and I was almost paralyzed with fear and anger at my old enemy. When you came back from death to tell me how beautiful it was, you threw me for a real loss."

"It's no loss, John. It's a gain, a plus. You don't have to hate death any more. He can be a friend. I know. Trust me, John."

"I accept your experience, Bets. I believe in heaven. And I would like to feel that death can be a friend. But I love it here so much. I love you and Brenda and my work and the outdoor life. I just can't believe that the next world will be as good. Tell me again what you saw."

Once more I told him the story of my death, remembering the details as if it had happened yesterday . . . the feelings of joy and lightness . . . the colors of grass, sky, jeweled walls . . . the glorious music . . . then the intoxication and purification of that intense yellow light. "It was a blinding light because I don't think I was supposed to see the Person of Jesus," I mused. "But how I felt His warmth."

"You said you wanted to go inside the city," John continued. "Why? What did you think you'd find there?"

"I wanted very much to go inside because it looked so beautiful and the music was, well, so heavenly."

"But beauty and music are here, too, Bets. Plus so much more. I've always heard that heaven was beautiful with wonderful music. What else did you see?"

"The Person of Jesus. His Presence excited me more than anything I had ever known. I felt I could learn from Him the answers to every question I ever had. I felt that He knew me better than anyone in the world and loved me completely in spite of my faults. It was His love that really got to me. I wanted so much to go inside and be with Him and worship Him."

John's eyes were now shining. He was more relaxed, and I sensed he was beginning to feel some of the intense love of Jesus I had felt.

Early the next morning before John was awake, I slipped out of bed, put on a warm robe, picked up my Bible and crept out on the balcony. The pink rays of the early morning sun filtered through the trees onto the dew-covered Florida campus. As I took deep breaths of the morning freshness, I thought back to John's and my conversation the night before. John's determination to know every detail of my walk with the angel had both stimulated me and made me uneasy. Did he feel he was going to die? He was facing a serious operation, but the doctors were optimistic. No, I concluded, John just yearned to be healed. He wanted his vitality back again.

Yet I needed to provide every possible kind of reassurance for him. I closed my eyes and sought again the Presence. "Jesus, is there anything more you have to tell me?"

The Lord had given me total recall of every phase of my time in heaven, except one. I joyously sang a song that was rendered in many parts and in several different languages by many other voices. At the time I understood the words and thought I would never forget them. Yet later I could not remember either the words or the melody.

As I prayed for an answer to this on my motel balcony, these words flashed before me:

You see through a glass darkly.

Quickly I turned to the well-known thirteenth chapter of First Corinthians on love. Carefully I read it over in my King James Version. With rising excitement I wrote down certain verses and studied them, at the same time keeping up my prayer dialogue.

For now we see through a glass darkly. . . . Our obvious condition in this world, Lord, is not to be able to see or understand the mysteries of the world to come.

But then face to face. You have already shown me that at death we come face to face with You, Lord.

Now I know in part; but then shall I know even as also I am known. We have partial knowledge now which will become full awareness in heaven. This must mean, Lord, that in Your City we will know everyone there, just as everyone there will know us. And in heaven we will have instant knowledge of all other languages (. . . *we shall be like him, for we shall see him as he is*—1 John 3:2). When I stood at Your gate, Lord, I had this knowledge; I knew the meaning of all the different words in all the different languages! But this knowledge was withdrawn once I returned to this world. I suppose it had to be this way, Lord, otherwise having such wisdom in this world would give me an exalted status.

For an hour I prayed and read His Word and was enriched by the bits of knowledge He dropped into my mind and heart. Then John awoke and we sipped coffee and prayed together.

Later that day we were sitting on the balcony watching the shadows of trees and buildings lengthen as the sun sank below the western horizon. John had gone through some heart tests in the morning, then had slept several hours in the afternoon. He was rested, eager to continue his questions.

"Years ago, Bets, the pastor in our church preached that we make our heaven or hell on earth. That made sense to me then. But not now. I've come to believe there is a heaven after this life. I'm just not sure I'm going to like it. I'll miss so many things. Sports, for example."

"What makes you think there'll be no physical activities in heaven?"

"What makes you think there will? I can't imagine playing ball in long flowing robes."

"The Bible says Heaven will be a busy, active place."

"I don't know that passage."

It was in the 65th chapter of Isaiah: *Therefore thus says the Lord God. . . . Behold, I create new heavens and a new earth. . . . They shall build houses and inhabit them; they shall plant vineyards and eat their fruit . . . for like the days of a tree shall the days of my people be, and my chosen shall long enjoy the work of their hands* (Isa. 65:13, 17, 21, 22).

We talked at length about the kinds of work there could be in God's City. John wanted to know other passages which promised life after death. I did some research and came up with the following:

Rejoice that your names are written in heaven (Luke 10:20).

In my father's house are many rooms; if it were not so, would I have told you that I go to prepare a place for you? (John 14:2).

He [God] will swallow up death forever, and the Lord God will wipe away tears from all faces (Isa. 25:8).

To the thief on the cross, Jesus said: Today you will be with me in Paradise (Luke 23:43).

And then there were those tremendous words I saw in block letters: *Whoever lives and believes in me shall never die* (John 11:26).

I could see that John had no real problem accepting the Bible promises. He just could not believe that the next world would be better than this one. What would there be to do?

"I can't point out any more specifics than what the Bible tells us," I replied. "In the singing I heard outside the gate I felt great joy, vitality, creativity, love, happiness, aliveness. It was anything but dull; perhaps peaceful in a way, but not a bland peacefulness. I had a definite feeling that the minute I entered those gates, I would begin a whole new learning process that would completely absorb every ounce of strength I possessed."

John's eyes were fixed on me intently. "I don't think I quite believed you that morning there in the hospital when you said you had been given a glimpse of eternity. I wanted to, but I just couldn't all of a sudden think kindly of something I had hated for so long. I was grateful that you were well again but I just could not believe that dying could be . . . well, good news."

"I'm sure it doesn't seem like good news to people here on earth who lose people they love," I replied. "I love life as much as you do, John. That hasn't changed. But I no longer see death as an end to life; it's the start of a new life. Life on earth is short; eternity is a long, long time. I'm just so grateful that I've been given a glimpse of where I'm going to be in the forever. And every fiber of my being tells me that if you love God and believe His promises, you have absolutely nothing to fear."

John's eyes suddenly filled with tears. I reached out my arms and he held me like he could never let me go.

Later that night we were sitting out on our small balcony again, holding hands and drinking in the sweet aroma of frangipani blooms. John was relaxed and romantically attentive. I confessed to him that I had never felt right about following Dr. Bherne's advice on contraceptives.

John was in quick agreement. "The Lord gave us His word on the subject before we had Brenda. He said He would pour His Spirit upon our seed, and His blessing upon our offspring. How much plainer can that be?"

I felt remorseful. "How wrong we were not to realize that God had an answer to this problem all along," I replied. With my contrition there came the gentle but sudden awareness that He was preparing me again for motherhood.

The tests went smoothly for John and the four days turned out to be the most wonderful period we had ever had together. There was time to talk, to rest, for making love, for prayer, time for absorbing Scripture together, to explore seafood restaurants, time to rediscover how much we cared for each other.

At the end of our second honeymoon, John made the decision to go ahead and have the operation. A date was set for May 12th, two months from then.

Five weeks later I was sitting on a low brick wall, lined with swaying palm trees, at the back of our home in Clearwater. I was having my first cup of coffee and thought to myself, "What a glorious April dawn! Thank You, Lord, for the beauty and fragrance of Your out-of-doors."

I now started each day with Jesus' name on my lips. This morning while meditating I was aware of a strangely sweet sensation. Like the whisper of a wonderful secret, it dawned on me . . . I was expecting!

"Lord, how exciting; but is it all right?" I wondered. Did I have something new to add to the needles of worry in my spirit about John?

It was a fragile moment. The sun was warm on my body. The birds were singing. God seemed to be caressing my troubled spirit, flooding me with His love. I was to depend upon Him for everything and He would be with me. His Spirit would fill me with strength; the healing work in my body was continuing. I was not to worry about the new life in my womb nor think about Dr. Bherne's warning; He would take care of it.

John was very sober when I went with him to the hospital; Mother and Dad were on hand, too, since they had moved to Florida earlier, Dad taking the pastorate of a small church in Palm Harbor nine miles away. Mother and Dad Upchurch were also present. Then the six of us had prayer together in John's room before the operation.

After the surgery the doctor appeared to tell us that all had gone well. His reassurance was premature. The operation was a success, but the surgeon had decided to use a new process of thread-type valve instead of the longer method of suture. The new thread closure let a blood clot slip through, causing paralysis on John's right side.

For days John lay in his hospital bed depressed, wanting to come home. Then through a registered nurse who lived next door, we equipped a bedroom in our home with the medical equipment John would need. The hospital approved our setup, and plans were made to bring him home.

At 9:30 on a Monday morning, Brenda and I arrived at the hospital to engineer the triumphant homecoming. As we entered the room, John was propped up in bed looking toward the door.

Brenda ran to him, "Daddy, you're going home." There was no reply. Something was wrong. John's eyes were open, peaceful, but glazed. Brenda tugged at his robe sleeve, "Daddy, it's really true . . . you get to go home." In a panic, I ran to the nurses' station to get help.

A doctor and a nurse soon rushed into the room with emergency equipment. It was too late. My thirty-six-year-old husband was gone. I was numb, plunged into darkness, only dimly aware of Brenda beside me, sobbing silently.

10

ALL THINGS COME TOGETHER

I T IS HARD for me to understand the blackness that came over me after John's death. I though I was prepared for this possibility. John and I had been given a beautiful time together at Gainesville where we saw clearly that God had permitted me a glimpse of His City so that I could share it with John.

Instead of acceptance and looking to God for further illumination, I became obsessed by post-mortem what-ifs. What if we hadn't moved to Florida? What if he had gone in for the operation two years earlier as the doctors advised? What if he had had it done at the Miami hospital? What if the doctor had not used the new nylon valve technique? The list went on and on, but nothing changed the medical fact that John had died and the cause of death was ventricular fibrillation.

The time with John's parents at the funeral was devastating. Oscar Upchurch—sad, dignified, courteous, distant. Dorothy Upchurch—grief-stricken, emotional, as always sharp with questions. She never put it into words, but I felt the accusation in her sorrowful dark eyes: "You never believed me, Betty, but I warned you this could happen."

At the grave site Mother Upchurch wept uncontrollably. I felt I could almost read her thoughts. "Why did it have to be Betty who recovered and my John who was taken?"

Brenda was sobbing too, a lovely blonde young beauty with a colt-like appearance, soon to enter her teens. Why did she have to be deprived of a father at such a crucial time in her life?

Gary, beginning to shoot up at twelve, hovered about me in a protective manner. "I'll come stay with you, Sis, and help out around the house," he said, his hand patting my arm just like John was always doing.

The reassurance of my parents and my brothers was strengthening, but no one could help me at the point of my greatest need. I felt deserted by the Lord. Let down. Yes—I'll admit it—betrayed. Ever since I had been cleansed and restored in His light, I had felt His Spirit dwelling in me. It had been a glorious, indescribably beautiful period. During the tornado He was there to guide me out of danger; in a hundred small daily crises He had been my rock and strength. But now, an expectant mother, I felt alone, desolate, abandoned, rebellious, angry.

John died on June 15, 1965. For two weeks I carried the grief, going no place, hiding at home. Instead of seeking strength and assurance from the Lord, I remembered the composure of Jackie Kennedy at the funeral of President Kennedy and was determined to put on a duplicate of her act. Pretending to be someone else, of course, never works.

It was Brenda who jolted me out of my self-pity. I had finally left home to go shopping one day at the supermarket. A teenage boy had carried two heavy sacks of groceries to the car for me. When I arrived home Brenda met me at the carport. I was sliding from under the steering wheel holding one of the overloaded bags.

"Mother, you should not lift that much weight. Let me carry it for you," she called.

"Don't fuss over me," I snapped back. "I'll do it myself."

"Mother, let me help. You must think of the baby." She grabbed one side of the sack and tried to pull it from my arms. I resisted.

Brenda suddenly became very stern. "Mother, let go of the sack! I can't carry it for you if you insist upon holding onto the sack!"

The dam broke inside me. Light poured into my mind. I let go, ran into the house, into my bedroom, dropped onto my knees and for the first time since John's death the tears came. For His Word once again flooded my heart, sparked by Brenda's sharp rebuke. There it was in bold letters:

Surely He has borne our griefs and carried our sorrows (Isa. 53:4).

"Oh, Jesus, I will let go of my heavy sack. Forgive me for holding it so tightly that I couldn't hear Your word or feel Your presence. I've let it all go right now, Lord. I am so tired of the burden. Please take it. Please come back to me. Please . . . please, Lord."

When I got up from my knees, the weight of depression was lifted. For the first time I began to see how completely John and I had been prepared for his passing.

Being able to share with John the beauty of death had helped my husband go into the next world unafraid. He would be met and escorted to the King's palace. There would be music which John loved, people he knew, unlimited time and space to be and do all he had ever dreamed about. Greatest of all would be the teaching and fellowship and love of the Lord Himself.

The suddenness of John's passing had temporarily blinded me to the gentle and loving way we had been brought to the moment of his death. Invalidism would have been agony for John, agony for those of us who loved him. God had been merciful. Now I fully understood John's rapt attention to my experience on the other side, his coming back to it again and again. "You say, Betty, that there was such a feeling of vigor and lightness. . . . You really did want to go inside that gate, didn't you?"

Several nights later God completed this healing by sending a special message to me through a dream. I was walking down a dusty path leading to a crude stone shed. I noticed the door was open and walked inside. There an elderly man wearing a cobbler's apron was molding some damp red clay into cups, urns, and pots. Behind him on the shelf were pieces of beautifully decorated pottery.

Suddenly a plain jar fell to the floor. The man, paying no attention to me, bent over and picked up the cracked vessel. While holding it gently, he reached into an urn nearby, dipping his fingers into warm molten liquid, and began to seal the broken vessel with the wax. He finished mending it and placed it back on the shelf behind him.

Then he saw me and smiled. "It is better to be a broken vessel, mended and sealed by the Holy Spirit and thus ready to serve, than a vessel without flaw, ornate and beautifully decorated, but unwilling to serve."

I awakened. Any doubts that I could ever be used of God again because of my flaws were gone. Tears of joy and repentance began to flow freely. I felt the warm wax of the Holy Spirit pour over my wounded spirit in healing power!

The crack that had come into my broken heart had been mended. Once again I had peace and joy in my heart.

Everything was right again between me and the Potter. I was ready and eager to be poured out for others in the Lord's service.

Filled with assurance that the block between myself and the Lord had been removed, the next morning I was on my knees determined to bring to His attention some of the unresolved matters that had been on my heart. I had scarcely begun my few words of petition when I felt His gentle correction: *You have always been a controlling woman, Betty. Now stop trying to manipulate Me and listen.*

This quieted me and the Holy Spirit began His teaching: *You have learned, Betty, how pride and resentment can cripple you. You have been freed of your ill feeling toward people like Art Lindsey, your prejudice toward the blacks, your love of material possessions. I cannot answer your prayers now as long as you hold unforgiveness toward your mother-in-law.*

Shortly thereafter I wrote a long letter to Dorothy Upchurch, parts of which I've reconstructed here from memory.

Dear Dorothy:

Ever since John's death I've been wanting to write you a letter and try to say some things that have been on my heart. The Lord is telling me that now is the time; that He wants to do some healing work in our relationship.

First of all, I want to confess that from the beginning of our marriage I felt very jealous of John's closeness to you and I resented the fact that you knew so much and I knew so little. But I was a stubborn and proud woman and felt that I was quite able to run our home, be a loving wife to John and a good mother to Brenda. The Lord has shown me in recent years that I need to depend much more on Him and much less on myself.

I was too grief-stricken to try and talk to you at the time of the funeral. I did not understand why the Lord spared me and took John. Lately I've stopped trying to understand theological issues and am content again to trust that God knows what He is doing. There is the wonderful assurance that John is with the Lord being more fulfilled than he ever was here on earth.

Please forgive me for the resentment I've held against you all these years and for every hurtful thing I've done to you. Since we both loved John so much I do feel the Lord wants us to heal our differences and bring our two families closer together.

Thank you for hearing me out. May God bless you and prosper your family.

With love,

It was several months before Mother Upchurch answered. Then she did, a sweet note. The relationship was restored.

As the seed which John planted in my body during our Gainesville honeymoon grew and developed, I fastened again unto God's promise that He would "bless our offspring" and overrule the gloomy medical prognosis. When John passed away, my faith had wavered. John had ignored the warning of his doctor and the doctor had been right. John had paid the price of living at an accelerated tempo.

Since John and I had gone against the advice of my doctor and I had become pregnant, would the doctor be proven right again? Would I bear a deformed baby?

When the dark cloud lifted, thanks to Brenda's sharpness with me, faith and hope returned. Dad, Mom, Brenda and I began to prepare for a happy blessed event sometime around the middle of December. The four of us began the countdown. "It will be born on Christmas Day—our gift to Jesus on His birthday," predicted my mother.

But in November our doctor began to doubt that it would be a full-term baby. Just before John's death I had nearly suffered a miscarriage. The early pregnancy months had been filled with such tension and hyperactivity that the doctor became increasingly uneasy as the weeks went by.

On November 27 he entered me into the hospital in Dunnedin, Florida. Labor began the next day. At 5:28 p.m. on November 28, a five-pound, two-ounce baby girl was born three weeks prematurely. We named her April Dawn because of my awareness early one April morning seven months before that God had created her.

November 28 was also Thanksgiving Day. Again, what a perfect timing He has! And how much we had to be thankful for! April Dawn was as normal and healthy and perfect a baby as this mother, with overflowing heart, could ask.

I can see now that all along God had been preparing me for new life. He did it by bringing me close to death so that I could view firsthand what a joyous experience it was. He restored my body and brought new life out of it in the form of a beautiful baby girl. God will always bring life to every situation.

Why God chose me—a selfish, proud, unloving person—for this unusual experience I'll never know. Perhaps, just as Joshua and Caleb went out to spy the land and brought back the grapes of Eschol (Num. 13:23), God let me spy out the heavenly city so that I could come back and tell everybody how great and beautiful it was. Perhaps he spared me so that I could reassure John that there is no reason to fear death, that he had a glorious adventure ahead of him, that Jesus was waiting to greet him with loving, open arms.

AFTERGLOW

THE CALL AWAY from Florida and to a new life in the west began with the death of my gentle and devout mother—Fern Perkins—on December 19, 1969. Several months later, Brenda began seriously thinking of attending a college the following September in Springfield, Missouri. Brenda, April Dawn, and I drove to Springfield to look over the school and enroll her, it if seemed right.

It was a low period for me. There was the recent loss of my mother, I had gone through almost five years of the loneliness of widowhood, and now I was having to face up to the fact that Brenda would soon be away at college.

Shortly after arriving in Springfield, we fell in love with and bought an old, three-story, twelve-room Victorian house, a hundred-year-old landmark. The girls and I began immediately restoring and redecorating the interior. We decided to stay on in Springfield, had our furniture and possessions shipped to us, and the girls enrolled in local schools.

At almost the same time we were led to settle in Springfield, one of God's special missionaries, Carl Malz, decided to move his family from Beirut, Lebanon, to Springfield. His wife

Wanda was terminally ill with cancer. Connie, their daughter, was thirteen. Carl had been overseas for many years in Egypt, served as President of the Southern Asia Bible College in Bangalore, India, and founded the Middle East Evangelical Theological School in Beirut in 1968.

Wanda Malz died several months after arriving in Springfield.

While teaching a Vacation Bible School class in church that next summer, I was attracted to a young teenage girl who was having trouble adjusting to her new home. Connie Malz and I had a grief we could share together—we had both recently lost our mothers.

It was Connie who introduced me to her father. Carl and I knew almost from the beginning that God had brought us together. Connie confirmed it when she confided to me, "You're the first lady I've met whom I'd like to have for my mother."

April Dawn the previous Christmas had asked, "Oh, God, give me a daddy for Christmas—a big 'un."

Carl Malz is six feet three inches tall and weighs 205 pounds. He and I were married the following June 3, 1971. Several months later Carl received a call to the Trinity Bible Institute in North Dakota to teach Foreign Missions. We were there for four years when Carl accepted a pastorate in Pasadena (outside Houston), Texas, where we now live and work.

Brenda did not enroll at the college in Springfield, but at Presbyterian College, Jamestown, North Dakota. There she fell in love with the son of her professor. She and Miles Millard Smart III were married in July 1974. Everyone calls him Bud. We tell people that "Bud went to college to make Bud-wiser, but Brenda went to college to get smart and did—Bud Smart."

Several years after Mother passed away, Dad moved to Kennard, Texas, a small town 159 miles north of Houston where his son Jim has a cattle ranch. Dad, at seventy, works on the ranch, teaches a Christian growth class at his church and handles a counseling ministry, giving him a full, balanced, rewarding life.

Meanwhile, Mother Upchurch and I continued our correspondence. She and Oscar had retired to a small place near Albany, Kentucky. I'll never forget the visit we made there in August 1976. Brenda, her husband, April Dawn, and I flew to the nearest airport and then rented a car to drive the additional 126 miles. Inside, I marveled at how important this visit was to me. When Mother Upchurch lived only a short seven blocks away when John and I were first married, I hardly ever went to visit her; now it was costing us almost a thousand dollars and I could hardly wait to see her and Oscar Upchurch.

It was almost sundown when we drove into the driveway of their small nature farm at the foothills of the Cumberland Mountains in Duvall Valley, Kentucky. From Mother Upchurch's letters I learned that they raised their own food through beef cattle, corn, grain, and a small orchard.

Dad Upchurch was on the porch of their five-room house, standing tall and straight, with hair now white, blue eyes faded, as he greeted us. Tears brimmed his eyes. Mother Upchurch burst forth from the kitchen, dark hair now full of gray, her step slowed, but the vitality still there. She hugged us, one by one. It was real. The love was genuine.

We sat down to a table groaning under home-grown food: a famous Kentucky smoked ham, homemade cornbread, homemade jelly, applesauce from fresh apples, fresh vegetables, milk, cheese. The next day was spent in talk and leisurely walks about the farm, while the two elderly people feasted their eyes on their two grandchildren. How important it is to keep these family ties, I thought to myself.

Before we left on the third day, Mother Upchurch presented me with several jars of blackberry jelly. Dad Upchurch whispered to me that back in June, when his wife knew we were coming, she had climbed the mountain paths in the area, picking fresh wild blackberries and making the jelly the old-fashioned way, slowly boiling the nectar together with sugar for hours until it had the right consistency.

That night back in our home I saw it: Dorothy Upchurch had always been the same sweet, thoughtful person I had seen that day. I had simply been too self-centered, jealous, and blind to see her as she really was. Why had I not been able to accept people as they were rather than always wanting to change them? Why could I not live fully and joyously in the present moment?

Now I knew! I had to die in order to live.

Joy Cometh in the Morning

O Lord my God, I cried unto thee, and thou hast
  healed me.
O Lord, thou hast brought up my soul from the
  grave: thou hast kept me alive, that I should not go
  down to the pit.
Sing unto the Lord, O ye saints of his, and give
  thanks at the remembrance of his holiness.
For his anger endureth but a moment; in his favour
  is life: weeping may endure for a night, but joy co-
  meth in the morning.
And in my prosperity I said, I shall never be moved.
Lord, by thy favour thou hast made my mountain to
  stand strong: thou didst hide thy face, and I was
  troubled.
I cried to thee, O Lord; and unto the Lord I made
  supplication.
What profit is there in my blood, when I go down to
  the pit?
Shall the dust praise thee? shall it declare thy truth?
Hear, O Lord, and have mercy upon me: Lord, be
  thou my helper.

Thou hast turned for me my mourning into danc-
ing: thou hast put off my sackcloth, and girded me
with gladness;
To the end that my glory may sing praise to thee, and
not be silent. O Lord my God, I will give thanks
unto thee for ever.

(Psalm 30:2–12, KJV)